PREHISTORIC HUNTERS of the BLACK HILLS

BY E. STEVE CASSELLS

Johnson Books: Boulder

Cover design: Joyce Rossi

ISBN 0-933472-96-X

LCCCN 86-80168

Printed in the United States of America by
Johnson Publishing Company
1880 South 57th Court
Boulder, Colorado 80301

CONTENTS

To Larry Agenbroad,
teacher extraordinaire,
who helped me to see the
Black Hills through new eyes

PREFACE

As a child, I ventured a few times into the Black Hills with my parents. My memories of those early visits involve carefree, exuberant swims in the hot mineral waters of Evans Plunge, shaking hands with a grandson of Chief Red Cloud, gazing in awe at the granitic faces on the east side of Mount Rushmore, and finding a few gold flecks in a prospector's pan at a roadside tourist attraction. All heady experiences for a youngster.

Much later I became an undergraduate biology student at Chadron State College, just over a stone's throw south of the Hills in Nebraska's panhandle. On a whim, I registered for an introductory geology course, and after half a semester of trying to remember the difference between an anticline and a syncline, a horst and a graben, and a stalactite and a stalagmite, I found myself in Professor Larry Agenbroad's car with several classmates, on our way to a geological tour of the Black Hills.

Ten hours later I realized something momentous had taken place inside my head. From a distance I had seen this black "blister" on the skin of the plains. Drawing nearer, I was able to comprehend the forces that had deposited and then carved through a series of progressively older river terraces that were stacked like levees along the inside of a big Cheyenne River bend. Then, as we entered through a water gap into the Hills, I saw the rough tilted Hogback sandstones, then the bare reddish "Racetrack" Valley, the flat-topped Limestone Plateau with its vertical white cliffs, and finally the puffy marshmallow-shaped intrusive granites that jutted up into the basin of the Central Core. In my mind's eye, I saw shaggy bison lumbering up through the water gaps into the grassy parks of the interior toward an unexpected rendezvous with ancient hunters who patiently lay in wait. It was at that point that my vocational goals began to shift slowly toward geology and archaeology.

Now, some twenty years later, I find I am still in awe of that pine-covered island, that refuge from the dry prairie sea, and I count myself fortunate to be among the few who have been able to conduct professional archaeological research within its confines.

This book on Black Hills archaeology is not intended primarily for professional archaeologists. Although I hope they will find it of some use as an overview, I had in mind more the curious resident and the uninitiated visitor, the captivated traveler who wants to know more about those who came before.

I hope that what I share here will be of value to you, the reader, that it will encourage you to pursue deeper studies and to develop a sense of responsibility toward our ancient heritage, prompting the desire to help protect it for the the benefit of future generations.

ACKNOWLEDGEMENTS

This book on Black Hills archaeology was possible only because of numerous individuals who were willing to help.

Photographs were generously provided by George Frison, Larry Agenbroad, Adrien Hannus, Jim Haug, Bob Alex, Mark Miller, Linea Sundstrom, Steve Sigstad, the Smithsonian Institution, the *Northern Wyoming Daily News*, the W.H. Over Museum, and the *Yankton Daily Press and Dakotan.* The superb pen and ink cultural reconstructions were rendered by Robin Farrington.

Those who provided invaluable counsel and information include Alice Tratebas, Bob Alex, George Frison, Lance Rom, Paul Miller, Linea Sundstrom, Jim Benedict, Michael McNierney, Pat Hofer, Robin Farrington, Mark Miller, and Adrien Hannus.

Finally, I wish to thank Michael McNierney and Barbara Mussil of Johnson Books for their confidence in me and for the excellent editorial assistance and design work.

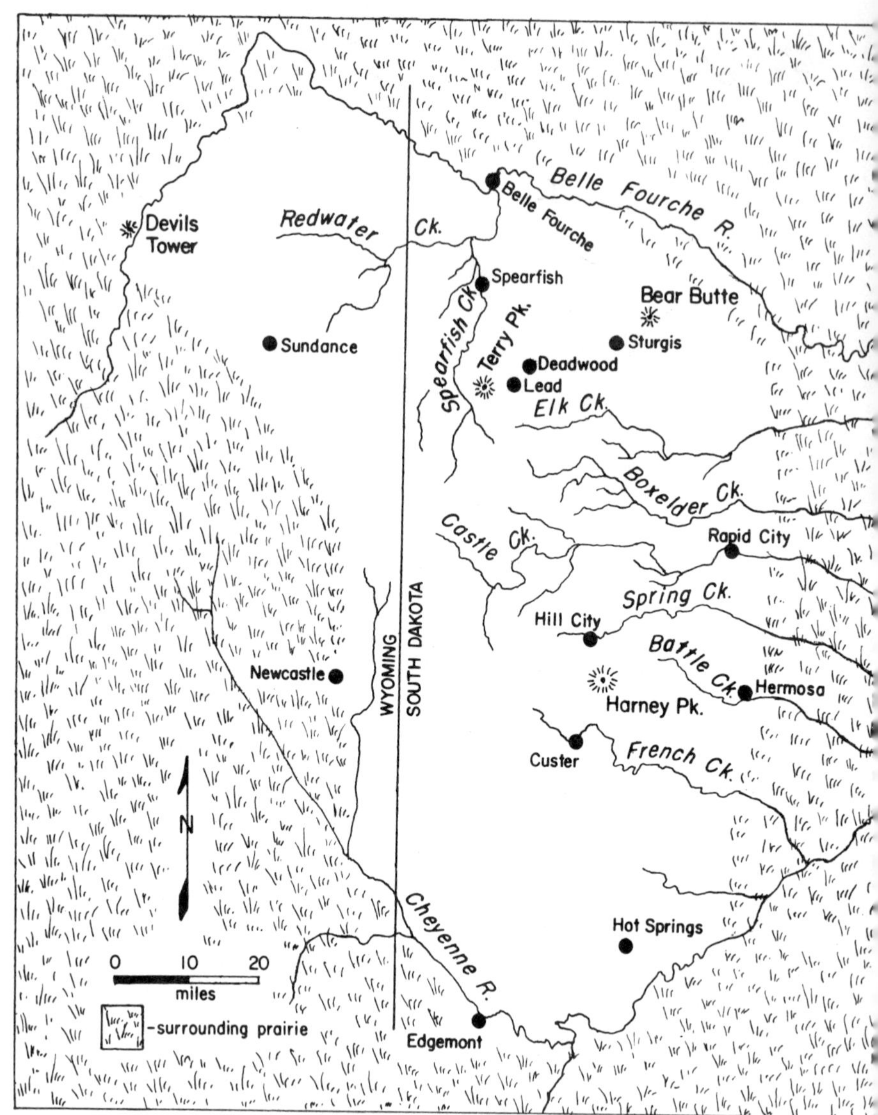

The drainage pattern for the Black Hills, with some topographic and community landmar

INTRODUCTION TO THE SCIENCE OF ARCHAEOLOGY 1

Agatha Christie, wife of British archaeologist Max Mallowan, once remarked that she enjoyed being married to him because the older she got, the better he liked her. It is true that archaeologists are interested in "old things," and to many of us, "the older the better."

To have been the first to break through the tomb wall and view the burial treasures of King Tutankhamun, at last exposed in all its splendor after so many centuries, must have been a thrilling experience for archaeologist Howard Carter in 1922.

In 1911 Howard Bingham climbed the lush green slopes of the Andes, far from the beaten path of humanity, and there, after seemingly endless efforts, he discovered the pristine Inca refuge city of Machu Picchu, nestled in the clouds at the top of the world.

In 1888 Colorado rancher Richard Wetherill and his brother-in-law, Charles Mason, were chasing cattle through a snowstorm on an unexplored pine-covered mesa. They stumbled upon an abandoned 13th century ruin hidden beneath the tan sandstone cliffs of what is now Mesa Verde National Park, and the mystery and majesty of the village they named Cliff Palace dramatically changed the lives of both the discoverers and their families. Today over half a million people a year are drawn to that mesa by the same forces that captured the Wetherills a century earlier.

Prehistory has had that effect on many people. They jump at the chance to see, to touch the remains of an earlier day. British archaeologist Stuart Piggott has called archaeology "the science of rubbish;" much of what prehistorians study is not "treasure" in the classic sense but the ordinary materials of the day, abandoned and discarded by the original owners.

But these are just "things," the materials of the former cultures (and thus often termed "material culture"). They are the concrete representations of past lifeways, but they are not themselves the lifeways. Archaeologists do not collect artifacts for any inherent value of an individual specimen. The archaeologist is not as interested in an arrowhead as in the Indian *behind* that arrowhead.

Archaeology is one of four divisions of the discipline known as anthropology. Perhaps we anthropologists are being too presumptuous when we claim that anthropology is the "study of Man," but that is the subject anthropology explores. All that has to do with humanity is fair game to the anthropologist. This goes beyond the more modest boundaries erected by scientists in sociology and psychology. Anthropologists study the nature and variability in fossil and modern human bodies (physical anthropology); the intricasies of human languages, with special emphasis on culture (linguistics); the details of human cultures throughout the world (cultural anthropology); and the specifics of human cultures as they have existed in the past (archaeology).

A cultural anthropologist searches out the patterns of culture—how humans collectively think and act. Research focuses on political, religious, economic, and legal systems, and kinship organizations, along with other related aspects of culture. With information gathered, the cultural anthropologist can then conduct cross-cultural comparisons and attempt to formulate hypotheses about why there are differences between cultures. Fieldwork generally requires the scientist to become immersed in the culture, taking part in rituals and daily activities, a technique known as participant-observation. The product of such research, generally a reasonably complete documentation of the particular culture, is called an ethnography, a book on the lifeways of the group.

The archaeologist hopes in the end to recover information similar to that sought by the cultural anthropologist. However, limitations prevent the prehistorian from gathering the data in the same ways. Participant-observation and interviews are clearly impossible, as the early inhabitants are gone. Although some comparative data may be obtained from modern groups with possible cultural links to the particular prehistoric population under consideration, ethnographic analogies can go only so far. Cultures change. Therefore archaeologists use systematic surveys to locate sites, and then employ meticulous excavating techniques to recover the maximum amount of data from the selected locales. Once the site has been excavated, the data requires analysis, and then this information is compared to that from other sites within the region and beyond. A published report of the findings is the final step in a long process.

The basic aims of archaeology are to reconstruct the lifeways and culture histories of prehistoric peoples, to identify culture change, and to construct possible explanations for it.

This is a difficult task, given the fact that most of the prehistoric material culture has been broken, scattered, mixed, or caused to deteriorate through adverse soil conditions. This challenge is being met by imaginative scientists who continually develop new techniques in excavation and analysis to salvage useful data from the remaining scraps of earlier human population.

Since even the most careful archaeologist generally "destroys" a site by excavating it, great effort is expended to fully document every potential artifact and feature through three-dimensional mapping, clear photography, and proper collecting and labeling techniques. Successful analysis depends on this.

Archaeology is an exciting science. It provides an avenue along which we can "travel through time," giving us a chance to attain a greater understanding of the variety of life experiences. It gives us a long time-line upon which we may test hypotheses about environmental change and cultural adaptation. Perhaps knowledge gained in this way may help us to learn from the past and avoid unnecessary complications and catastrophes that could conceivably end humankind as we now know it.

However, archaeologists are sometimes accused of overstating the importance of the discipline.But just as the *Mona Lisa* is of great value to us, so are the findings of archaeology. Great works of art contribute to the fullness of our lives. They enrich us and help us to better appreciate the world as a whole. In the same way, though archaeology's contribution to humanity may not be quantifiable, directly save lives, or make our daily tasks easier, it is of great worth. To visit an archaeological site is to be transported across the ages, to feel, if only for a moment, past lifeways. We can see both continuity and change through time, and can better sense our place on earth.

References

On an introduction to archaeology:

Fagan 1978; Trigger 1968; Deetz 1967

On culture and cultural anthropology:

Kluckhohn and Kelley 1945; Kroeber and Kluckhohn 1952

On archaeological methods:

Hester, Heizer, and Graham 1975; Joukowsky 1980

DATING TECHNIQUES 2

Archaeologists are often criticized by people outside the field for what they see as the cavalier attitude toward the very old dates archaeologists work with. How can anyone be so certain about these dates? The critics are inclined to believe that archaeologists are in the same class with government economists who throw around numbers so big they are meaningless to most people.

It is true that archaeologists often work with the far past. They are comfortable with African finds dating several million years ago. (Here in the New World, our oldest well-accepted sites are relatively recent at slightly over 11,000 years old.) But the dates are not arbitrary, nor are the methods of reaching them casual or sloppy.

Still, there are those who question the reliability of current dating methods. This is not necessarily bad. No science advances without critics who take its theories and methodologies to task. An elementary explanation of some of the more basic dating methods that can be applied to Black Hills sites, along with the rationales behind them with hopefully make the information in following chapters more meaningful.

We live in an exciting time for archaeology. Beginning

in the 1920s and rapidly gaining momentum during the 1950s, the development of significant dating techniques has allowed insight into prehistoric periods never before possible. But physicists, chemists, and archaeologists working in the field have not been content to rest on their laurels. Refinements and innovations are still going on at such a rate that future generations of archaeologists will likely find it possible to look back at our "modern" methods and marvel that we were able to find out *anything* chronologically with our prehistoric samples. Until that time we must remain content with current levels of sophistication. They have proved to be extremely useful tools in understanding antiquity.

Relative Dating

Relative dating is the simplest method. If one were to say that Boston is older than Chicago, that would be an expression of relative age. No calendrical date would be needed to know which came first.

In archaeology, relative dates are used in sites where other dating techniques cannot be used, or before time-consuming dating processes have been completed and the results returned to the archaeologist. According to a geological principle known as the law of superposition, older materials occur in the ground below younger, shallower ones. This assumes, as is normally the case, that soils and sedimentary rock formations are originally laid down as horizontal layers, building up through time by an accumulative process.

As stratigraphic sequences are documented in a number of sites, a broader knowledge can be gained about cultural succession in a particular region. Later, if calendrical dating techniques can be used on similar finds elsewhere, these dates can be inferred to fit into the original relative sequence. The calendrical dates can be checked against the undated cultural ordering to see if discrepancies occur.

Radiocarbon Dating

Determining the age of a site through the analysis of radiocarbon (carbon 14 or C14) found in organic matter is the most common technique used in the New World today. It is very practical because most sites contain something organic (once living), whether it be wood or charcoal from once- standing structures or from old fires (the most preferred), bones from a butchering station or scraps tossed aside after a meal, or just black, highly-organic soils. Recent technological advances have widened the technique's applicability. Previously a teacup to a teaspoon full of carbon was required; now something no larger than a pencil eraser is adequate. The use of carbon 14 (C14) dating is very appropriate for North and South American archaeologists, as this technique is reasonably accurate on samples up to 50,000 years old, and the known human presence in this hemisphere is considerably less than this.

Radiocarbon dating was the brainchild of Dr. Willard Libby during the 1940s while he was a researcher at the Institue of Nuclear Studies in Chicago. His findings were eventually regarded as so significant that he was awarded the Nobel Prize in Chemistry in 1960.

Libby began by noting that cosmic radiation produces neutrons which react with nitrogen 14 to bring about the formation of carbon 14 isotopes. He assumed that the C14 then oxidizes into carbon dioxide, blends into the atmosphere, and is then dispersed rapidly around the world with normal air movements. Plants take in the C14 with the CO_2 and retain it at a predictable level that remains in equilibrium throughout each organism's life. Since C14 is radioactive, it decays at a given rate (a half-life of 5,730 ± 40 years). When absorption ceases at the organism's death, the level of C14 begins to diminish since there is no additional C14 intake to maintain the balance. Half-life decay

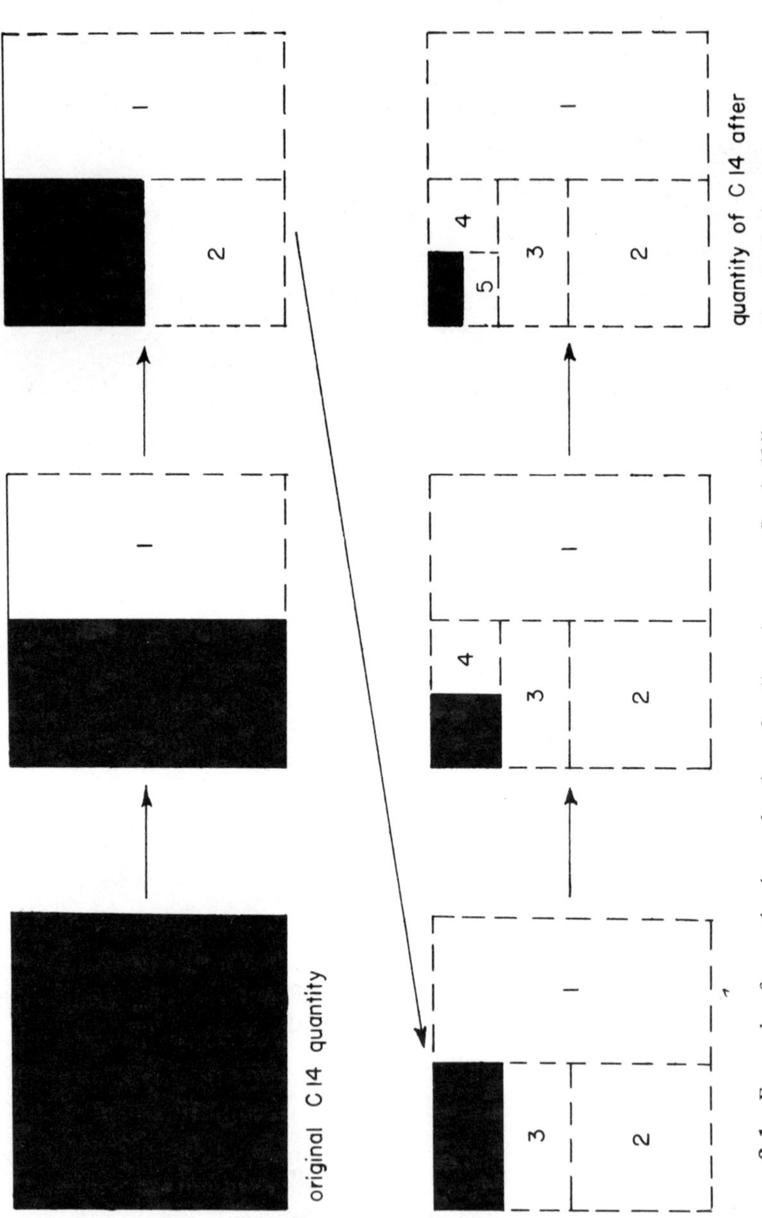

2-1 Example of quantitative reduction of radiocarbon over five half-lives.

does not mean that the radioactive isotopes will be fully exhausted after two half-lives. Instead, each half-life reduces the total *remaining* isotopes by one-half; two half-lives, therefore, leave one-fourth of the original quantity, rather than an amount approaching zero. In the case of radiocarbon, nine half-lives (slightly over 50,000 years) reduce the number of isotopes to such a small quantity that there would be little accuracy in any further measurement.

A carbon sample in the laboratory is converted into gas (carbon dioxide, methane, or acetylene), and the isotopes are then counted in a device similar to function to a Geiger counter.

Inorganic matter, such as rocks, cannot be dated with the radiocarbon technique. Theoretically any once-living organism, plant or animal, can be dated, although some materials, such as shell, do not work well for a number of reasons. Charcoal is highly reliable, readily available in a site, and as a result, is the most common material dated by the radiocarbon method.

This is not to say that radiocarbon dating is without its problems. Carbon has not been present in the atmosphere at a constant rate through the past 50,000 years, so plants and animals have absorbed varying amounts of the element depending on when they lived. However, once these fluctuations were discovered, cross-checking was possible by the use of tree-ring dating and other approaches. With the plotted results, a closer fit has now been made between radiocarbon years and calendar years.

Archaeologists and dating labs have to be constantly aware of the possibilities of contaminating carbon samples. Sources of contamination vary widely, but the most common are the mixing of carbon from younger or older levels, modern plant rootlets, or extremely old coal that may have been naturally present in the site. Any of these would result in a date far too old or young. With the current level of consciousness about the potential problems, however, great care is usually taken to assure the reliability of the datable samples.

Some critics argue that radiocarbon dating is not very accurate because there is always an error factor expressed behind the date, such as 10,000 ± 130 B.P., indicating a date probably lying somewhere within 130 years before or after 10,000 years ago. It is true that some other dating is more accurate (specifically tree-ring dating, a technique not yet applicable to Black Hills sites), but having a date within a relatively resticted age range is perfectly adequate for most archaeological work. That radiocarbon dating is not very expensive (average of about $200.00 a sample in 1985) and is generally analyzed and reported by the dating lab in a few weeks, makes it the most reasonable chronological tool available to North American archaeologists at present.

Other Dating Techniques

There are a number of other means that can be employed to learn the age of an archaeological site. Tree-ring dating, mentioned previously, is without a doubt the most accurate method available for prehistoric sites. However, the "reader" of tree rings has to have a good knowledge of the specific region in order to interpret a tree ring series, and preservation of prehistoric samples has to have been good. For that reason, the American Southwest is the only area where the technique is presently used on a widespread basis. The Black Hills lack good preservation, and the climate is so variable that several different tree ring growth patterns are present, making even the dating of century-old log cabins difficult at present.

Obsidian hydration, a method of measuring the accumulation of water on the outside of obsidian (volcanic glass) tools is a relatively new technique still subject to much experimentation. It is most used in conjunction with C14 dating for cross-check purposes. Few obsidian tools have been found in the Black Hills, thus eliminating it from any practical use there.

Archaeomagnetic dating is an interesting approach that focuses on ancient fire hearths containing magnetic particles (e.g. iron) in the clay of the feature. With the knowledge that the magnetic poles are dynamic, and that previous locations of the poles have been plotted, the archaeologist carefully takes a clay sample from a hearth, accurately noting its orientation in the ground first. In the lab, the alignment of the magnetic particles in the hearth clay is compared to the modern compass alignment with the North Pole, the assumption being that when the hearth was last fired, the clay was heated, and the iron in it was "freed" and lined up with the North Pole as it was then. The difference between then and now, when applied to the known polar migration, can determine when the early people last huddled around the fire. As with obsidian hydration, this method is fairly new, and continued refinement is taking place to perfect it and make it more applicable to prehistoric site dating. Although this approach would be perfectly acceptable for Black Hills sites, it has not, to my knowledge, been used there yet.

Thermoluminescence, a dating technique based on the principle that pottery, once fired in a kiln, will release energy when reheated. The amount of the reheated glow is proportional to the length of time since the last heating. The technique has not been used in the Black Hills yet, but it would be a reasonable approach, especially in concert with C14 dating.

Summary

Dating sites and building broad cultural chronologies for a region are two of the most difficult and yet most important aspects of archaeology. Improper collecting techniques, leading to a dating error, can unnecessarily clutter up and complicate the archaeological record for generations, but information from a well-dated site can be priceless for future investigators.

REFERENCES

On various dating techniques:

Hester and Grady 1982; Hester, Heizer, and Graham 1975; Suess 1965.

ENVIRONMENTAL SETTING
3

Geology

The Black Hills have been aptly described as a "blister on the Great Plains." Lying across the present South Dakota—Wyoming border, they rise 2,000 to 4,000 feet above the surrounding prairies.

The Black Hills were formed by a series of complex geological processes that began as early as the Precambrian era, perhaps 2.5 billion years ago.

At that time the land was under an inland sea, a source of extensive and heavy sediment deposition. Perhaps in conjunction with convection cells from the earth's interior, these sediments began to subside, forcing magma in the earth to rise. This intrusion of heat, along with massive pressures, caused overlying sediments to metamorphose into schist, slate, and quartzite. By the Cambrian period, 600 million years ago, erosion had cut down these first Black Hills.

Between the Cambrian and Tertiary periods (600 to 65 million years ago), a cycle of alternating updoming and sea inundation was responsible for additional deformation of the local strata and increased deposits of marine sediments.

It is thought that near the end of the Cretaceous period

(around 65 million years ago), just before the onset of the Tertiary, the inland sea receded for the last time.

Sometime during the Tertiary, massive mountain building took place throughout the region. This event is termed the Laramide Orogeny. Plate tectonics scientists think it coincided with the separation of the North American plate from the European plate, at which time the Atlantic Ocean was created in the gap. Not only were the Black Hills raised, but so was the present Rocky Mountain chain. No exact date can be placed on the Black Hills updoming, but it happened sometime between the end of the Cretaceous (65 million years ago) and the middle of the Eocene epoch (around 35 million years ago).

Those formations on the outer rim of the Hills are among the youngest rocks, while the granite, schist, slate, and quartzite in the central areas are the oldest. Near the northern part of the Hills, a number of igneous intrusives of the Tertiary period (e.g. Devils Tower, Bear Butte) are evidences of this final updoming.

Topography

There are four major components of Black Hills topography. These are (from oldest to youngest and from the center out) the *Central Core*, the *Limestone Plateau*, the *Red Valley*, and the *Hogback Ridge*.

The Central Core (also known as the Central Area or the Interior) is roughly 60 miles north-south by 25 miles east-west. It extends from the Pringle area south of Custer up to the vicinity of Deadwood in the north. All of the sedimentary overburden there has either been eroded away after being weakened and cracked by the updomings or has been metamorphosed by the Precambrian intrusives into the schist, slate, and quartzites that now are exposed there. What is striking are the granite mountains known as the

Harney Range. Included in the range are Harney Peak (elev. 7,242 feet) and the famous Mount Rushmore. Spectacular pinnacles, such as the Needles, are also part of this Precambrian granite formation. Numerous outcrops of schist, slate, and quartzite enclose the granite on all but the east side and make up the bulk of the Central Core's surface geology.

Encircling the Central Core is the Limestone Plateau. Composed primarily of Pahasapa Formation limestone, it rises abruptly, in some places up to 800 feet above the floor of the Central Core. Many springs with high discharge flow from the base of the limestone: water percolates down through the formation and meets less permeable rock below, which forces the water to move laterally to the surface. The Limestone Plateau varies in width from its maximum of about 15 miles on the west side of the Hills, down to about two miles or so on the east. Extending outward from its contact with the Central Core, the Limestone Plateau runs in relatively flat terrain toward the Red Valley.

This valley, known also as the "Racetrack," is a relatively narrow, unforested depression created by the erosion of the

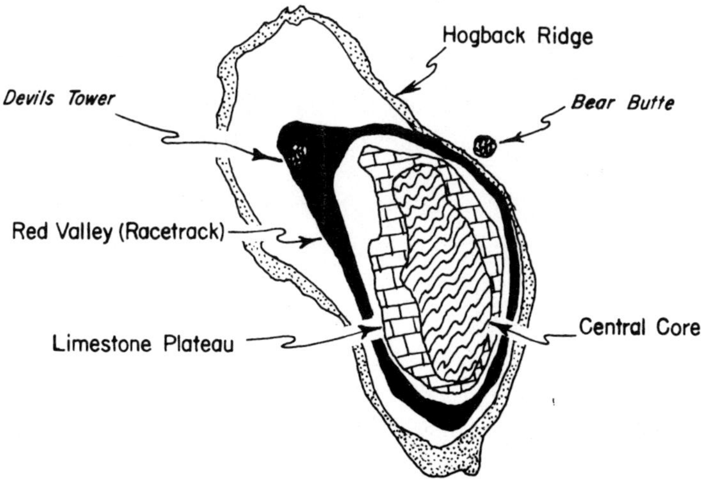

3-1 Simplified geologic/topographic map of the Black Hills.

softer red shales of the Spearfish Formation. The name "Racetrack" describes the fact that it encloses the inner Hills much like a circular track would.

Outside of Red Valley is the Hogback Ridge, a series of tilted sandstones of the Lakota and Fall River formations. The Hogback Ridge is up to several miles wide in the southern Hills but much narrower on the east.

The Hogback Ridge is the outermost feature of the Black Hills, rising out of the plains at an ever increasing angle, and then terminating with an abrupt escarpment on its inner face, adjacent to the Red Valley.

Streams exit the Black Hills through "water gaps," the narrow cuts in the Hogback that served as principal entry points into the Hills for humans, as well as for wild game such as bison. They still function today as routes for human traffic as many highways follow their courses.

In the northern Hills are a number of conspicuous igneous intrusives that are among the more recent geological phenomena in the area. As part of the last updoming there, they are of Tertiary age. Among them are the well-known Devils Tower, Bear Butte, and Terry Peak.

Stone for Prehistoric Hunters

Those early hunters that frequented the Black Hills survived primarily at a stone age level of technology. They were apparently well acquainted with sources of raw material for tool manufacture.

A number of exotic lithics have been brought to the Black Hills. There are four major outside sources: Spanish Diggings in Wyoming; the Powder River Basin in Wyoming and Montana; Knife River in North Dakota; and the Badlands of South Dakota. Local quarries are known from the Hills as well. Most, such as the famed Flint Hill (39FA49), are located along the Hogback. Some others have been found toward the interior, especially on the Limestone Plateau.

Spanish Diggings, an area that has been extensively quarried for millennia, contains several stone types, including a fine-grained quartzite. This quartzite, often tan to yellow in color, can be confused with quartzites from the southern Black Hills. Spanish Diggings quartzite comes from the Hartville Uplift of Wyoming, near Lusk; the southern Hills type, known as Hogback quartzite, comes from the Cloverly Formation. Considerable analysis has been necessary to distinguish between them.

A popular material of the area is porcellanite, a dull-gray to red silicate that originates north and west of the Black Hills. This material was originally shale that was later changed (metamorphosed) by close contact with burning subterranean coal seams. Fused glass and vitreous porcellanite were formed by the same process, though they are the products of greater heat, with fused glass being exposed to the highest temperatures of them all. Fused glass has been confused at times with obsidian. The actual source for any particular artifact of porcellanite, vitreous porcellanite, or fused glass is difficult to isolate, as there are broad coal formations from central North Dakota and northwest South Dakota west to Wyoming and Montana. The right conditions for porcellanite exist throughout the area. Perhaps the nearest known source to the Black Hills is the Powder River Basin, around 100 miles to the northwest. This source area has also been termed the Fused Shale Beds.

A popular silicate used by Black Hills hunters is called Knife River Flint, a translucent chocolate-brown chalcedony known to have been quarried along the Knife River of west-central North Dakota. Its widespread occurance in sites across the Great Plains suggests its popularity as a trade item.

East of the Black Hills are the Badlands, a large block of eroded shales and other sediments. Outcropping there are various chalcedonies known as Flattop and Plate chalcedony. Flattop chalcedony is dark brown and translucent. Chert inclusions in it, along with a distinctive cortex, separates it from a similar appcaring Knife River Flint. Plate Chalcedony, named for its common occurance in thin plates, is white to gray to pinkish gray.

Aside from the exotic lithic sources, a number of local quarries have been identified, and the raw materials have been given specific names.

Flint Hill and Battle Mountain, both in the southern Hills, are well-known sources for Hogback quartzite, a fine-grained variety occuring in the Cloverly Formation.

Deadwood quartzite, a coarse-grained dark red or orange quartzite, can be found at a number of outcrops in the southern Hills.

Pahasapa chert displays a wide variety of colors and textures. Coming from the Pahasapa Formation, it includes a tan to yellow dendritic jasper often mistaken for a similar type from the Spanish Diggings quarries.

Gypsum Springs chert, a purple fine-grained silicate that occurs as flattened nodules in the limestone of the Gypsum Springs Formation, is difficult to separate from the purple and red Minnelusa cherts from the Minnelusa Formation. Minnelusa cherts also occur in white, gray, tan, yellow, and orange.

The location of quarry sites are not as predictable as camp sites. They occur where the proper geologic formation exists and often the outcrops of suitable material appear on ridgetops. Since the silicates and their associated matrices are relatively resistent, it can be expected that a number of quarries will be on high ground. Some cutbanks (eroded banks generally along streams) may have exposed lithic sources in their stratigraphy.

It should be understood that detailed comparative petrographic studies are lacking for many lithic quarries, and as a result, identification of specific lithics should be considered as tentative. One must realize the difficulty of making field identifications of lithic types, even under the best of circumstances. And, within both the archaeological and geological communities, more than one common name may be used for the same lithic type, such as agate/chalcedony or red chert/jasper. The system has yet to be fully standardized.

Climate

The abrupt altitude change from the prairie to the Black Hills forces moisture-laden air masses, moving in from the north and west, to rise upward. This brings about a cooling and contracting of the air mass that "squeezes out" the rain and snow onto the Hills. Given this relatively abundant moisture in the Hills, plant life otherwise not compatible with plains conditions can thrive.

There are two climatic zones in the Black Hills. These are the Northern Hills and Southern Hills zones. From Deerfield on the south to Spearfish on the north, the Northern zone is significantly cooler and receives higher annual precipitation. The Deadwood-Lead area averages 29 inches of moisture a year, compared to 19.3 in Custer. The growing season in Deadwood is 107 days, compared to 142 in Hot Springs. The surrounding prairies receive only 14-17 inches of moisture per year.

Plant and Animal Life

Paha Sapa, in the Sioux tongue, means Black Hills (*Sapa*—black, *Paha*—hills), an indication of its color from afar, as well as its prominence above the otherwise flat landscape. Others have described it as a "forested island in a grassland sea."

The Black Hills can be divided into four primary plant

zones: the Rocky Mountain Coniferous Forest; the Northern Coniferous Forest; the Grasslands; and the Deciduous Forest.

The Rocky Mountain Coniferous Forest, covering the greatest area of the Hills, is dominated by the ponderosa pine. Ponderosa pine is tolerant of heat and low moisture, as well as of thin, rocky soils. The pine concentrates along the higher elevations, while mixed grasses dominate the open valley floors. This forest type is usually not extremely dense, although some stands of unthinned "dog-hair," tight clusters of stunted trees, do exist. The open nature of ponderosa growth allows for an understory of ground juniper, kinnikinnik and bearberry. Aspen tend to grow in open or disturbed areas. The limber pine and the lodgepole pine grow in limited stands as well.

The second plant zone, the Northern Coniferous Forest, is primarily limited to the Northern Hills climatic zone and to cooler canyons in the higher elevations of the Harney Range farther to the south.

A principal species in this complex is the white spruce. The Black Hills is its southern limit in this hemisphere, isolated from its primary range hundreds of miles to the north. Associated with the white spruce are a variety of plants that contribute to a lush vegetative understory. These include ferns, moss, lichens, and a number of flowers and grasses. Although in limited numbers, paper birch occurs in some of the cooler, moisture regions. Aspen flourishes on park edges and in disturbed areas.

The Deciduous Forest is made up of a variety of trees and shrubs. Among them are bur oak, American elm, green ash, box elder, and eastern hop-hornbeam. Cottonwood and peach-leaved willow dominate the streamback communities in the low elevations on the margins on the Hills but disappear toward the interior, where aspen, paper birch, and shrubs take over.

In the northern parts of the Hills, a more varied and widespread deciduous complex thrives, due to the increased moisture.

The Grasslands complex surrounds the Black Hills, having adapted to the more arid climate there. Primarily it is what could be called a mixed-grass grassland consisting of species from both the eastern tall-grass grasslands and the more western short-grass grasslands.

Within the Black Hills are a number of "high prairies" among the dense forest stands. Several, such as the Gillette Prairie and Reynolds Prairie (near Deerfield) and Danby Park (near Custer), are quite extensive. Others, especially on the Limestone Plateau, are more localized as minor meadows. Explanations for this have so far not been totally satisfactory. It does appear, however, that different soils are at least one factor.

Modern animals in the Black Hills include a diverse assortment of temperate climate species. Many were economically significant to both aboriginal and historic groups that frequented the area. Among them are the coyote, elk, mule deer, white-tailed deer, and black bear. The bison was important during both prehistoric and historic times but was nearly exterminated during the late 1800s. Bison can now be found in Wind Cave National Park and Custer State Park, as well as in some commercial ranching operations. Migratory waterfowl move through the Hills seasonally. Reptiles include turtles and snakes, the only poisonous species being the prairie rattlesnake.

Mammoth elephants once lived in the Black Hills, although at present there is no hard evidence they were actually hunted inside the Hogback Ridge. In 1974 construction on the south side of Hot Springs revealed mammoth bones in a sinkhole in the Red Valley. During prehistoric times (around 26,000 years ago) water lay in the bottom of this sinkhole, and the sides, steep and soft, would have effectively

3-2 Excavated skull of Columbian mammoth with ivory tusks at the Hot Springs Mammoth Site. (Larry Agenbroad)

trapped large beasts that dared to enter and drink. Between 1974 and 1983, Dr. Larry Agenbroad (Northern Arizona University) excavated the remains of at least 34 Columbian mammoths, a camel, a great short-faced bear, and a number of smaller mammals. Only 15% of the site has been excavated to date, and the results are open for the public to view.

The Black Hills are a land of immense beauty and complexity. They hold within their boundaries a heritage going back billions of years to a time when the area first began to separate from its watery surroundings. It has become a haven, not only for human populations, but also for a wide number of plant and animal species, many of which could not survive outside of the Hogback Ridge. It has provided a rich backdrop for the cultural parade that began at least 11,000 years ago.

References

On Black Hills geology:
Gries and Tullis 1955.
On Black Hills topography:
Darton and Paige 1925; Froiland 1978.
On raw lithic sources:
Tratebas n.d., 1978; Fredlund 1976; Frison 1974; Agenbroad 1978; Clayton et al. 1970; Haug 1979; Cassells 1980.
On Black Hills climate:
Froiland 1978.
On Black Hills plant and animal life:
Froiland 1978; Turner 1974; Pettingill and Whitney 1965; Johnson and Nichols 1982.
On the Hot Springs Mammoth site:
Agenbroad 1977.

4-1 Clovis hunters close in for the kill of a mammoth mired in the mud of a waterhole. (Robin Farrington)

THE PALEO-INDIANS
4

The sun rose, coating the countryside with an orange glow, and the cold air left a light frost on the landscape. A small herd of mammoths began stirring in a hollow of the landscape. Led by a massive bull, the three cows and two calves moved slowly as they grazed on the browning grass.

A mile away, a group of nine skin-clad hunters lay in wait. They had gathered together from three separate bands this fall to cooperate in a hunt, all hoping for enough food to divide among them and the more than forty mouths waiting in their camps. If there was meat from a kill, it could be cut into strips and dried, extending the supply into the winter months.

By noon the sun had warmed the region considerably. The air began to feel more like summer than fall. The mammoths, having eaten the tall grasses all morning, picked up their meandering pace. Locating a familiar game trail, they began walking single file, the youngest cow stopping occasionally to call back her errant calf. With the smell of water in the air, the tusked column cleared the rise and saw the water hole. Reeds and cattails encircled the pool. A dire wolf, startled by the advancing herd, made a sharp snort and quickly trotted over the hill in the opposite direction.

The hunters learned of the approaching mammoths from a lookout who had been watching their movements since dawn. The men were all placed to the south and east of the pond, as a slight breeze was blowing from the northwest, and the mammoths were walking in with the wind at their backs.

The column stopped as the big bull surveyed the terrain, raising his trunk majestically, searching for an enemy scent. There was none.

They walked down the gentle slope to the mud flats where their feet sank deeper and deeper into the mud. The bull stood watch while the others inched their way into the water. The calves were soon up to their necks, playfully blowing water out their trunks. The pool was churned in turmoil as they all milled around, drinking and bathing with apparent glee.

Then the bull trumpeted, trunk arched above a gleaming set of curved ivory tusks. The hunters had begun to disperse, and as two of them circled to the north, their scent reached the vigilant guardian of the herd. He whirled, and the herd instantly became still and silent. There was nothing out of the ordinary to be seen, but to catch the odor of humans was a fearful experience. They all became restless.

The bull caught sight of the two hunters on the rise, and with a mighty bellow, charged their position. The hunters ran, but with the south now unguarded, the other men moved quickly, reaching the pond's edge and surrounding the herd on three sides. Spears were launched, with several finding their mark, although the thick gray hides prevented the points and shafts from penetrating to lethal depths. The cows and calves began to leave the water, but the thick black mud held their feet and legs, allowing only a slow retraction of one leg at a time. Their retreat was sluggish. A second fusillade of spears filled the air, one hitting the lower spine of the youngest cow. Her hindquarters went limp and dropped. As the hunters closed in, the other mammoths emerged onto the bank and moved off to the north, spear shafts dangling out of their sides at odd angles. The smallest calf, confused and distressed at his mother's predicament, came back to her and was caught between the men. Rapid thrusts of their stone-tipped spears severed his spine as well, and he collapsed.

With most of the herd on the hilltop and out of immediate danger, the bull stood in front. His ears stood out to the sides and his head was high. Shaking his tusks, he made a mock charge, trying to frighten the copper-colored men away from the downed pair, but to no avail. Then, with much trumpeting and foot stamping, they turned and lumbered away.

The cow and calf were now dead. The men detached the forshafts from their spears so that each point could serve as a knife with a wooden handle. They pounced on the cow and calf, opening their sides and feasting on warm liver. With a diet the last two weeks of only a few roots, some chubby prairie dogs, and a rattlesnake, these hunters could finally feel the possibility that their families would be fed abundantly until at least the next moon.

Sending the youngest hunter back to alert the camps many miles away along the banks of the Cheyenne River, the men began skinning and butchering the beasts. The hides, too thick for clothing, could be used for sandal soles. Much of the meat, cut out in large muscle packets, was to be stripped and dried, but some would be cooked on the spot. Sinew was peeled off the joints to be dried and then separated into long strips for sewing and binding. Some of the leg bones were broken open. The marrow inside tasted good, and the bone fragments made good butchering wedges, cleavers, knives, and points.

When all the families finally arrived and a new camp was established, the once quiet waterhole became a hub of activity. Spirits were high as the survival of the bands was assured for the time being. Meat was passed out along prescribed lines of distribution, handed over from one relative to another until everyone had their fair share and all the meat was gone.

That night, as the campfires crackled on the prairie, some of the younger hunters daubed their shoulders with yellow clay and performed a dance of celebration, acting out the parts of the elephant herd and the hunters. The actors recounted the day in the dance, perhaps embellishing some events a little. The children sat watching, mesmerized, and old men drew their robes more tightly about their shoulders, smiled, and dreamed.

On To The New World

Prehistory dawned in the Americas when small bands of Asian nomads invaded the immense but unpopulated Western Hemisphere between 15,000 to 20,000 years ago, or perhaps earlier. The time of their arrival is the subject of much controversy within professional circles, with favorite dates being as late as 12,000 to 14,000 or as early as 40,000 or more years ago.

What is not controversial is that the human presence here is relatively recent. In other words, the humans who entered the continent were fully modern, not of the Neanderthal or earlier forms. It is also known that the migrations were from Asia.

Since these early hunters and gatherers came on foot and because North America is currently separated from the Asian continent, there is the question of how these people arrived. In answering this, we receive aid from geological studies—specifically glaciology.

From about three million years ago until perhaps 10,000 years B.P. (before present), the more northern and southern portions of the world were under the influence of the Ice Age, known otherwise as the Pleistocene. This period, colder than at present, was a dynamic time during which massive continental ice sheets built up in both the Old and New Worlds. We know of at least four major building events (advances), each separated by at least partial melting (recessions). Because the world is a closed system with a finite quantity of water available, when moisture became tied up in the ice, there was a reduction in the primary water source, the ocean. Thus, as a result of each glacial advance, sea levels dropped significantly, exposing the continental shelves and portions of the deeper sea floors. At the peak of glacier building, sea levels dropped worldwide as much as four hundred feet or more.

With this in mind, it is interesting to examine the ocean where it separates Asia from Alaska, a place known as the Bering Strait. The sea floor there is quite shallow, at some places less than one hunded feet in depth. If the present

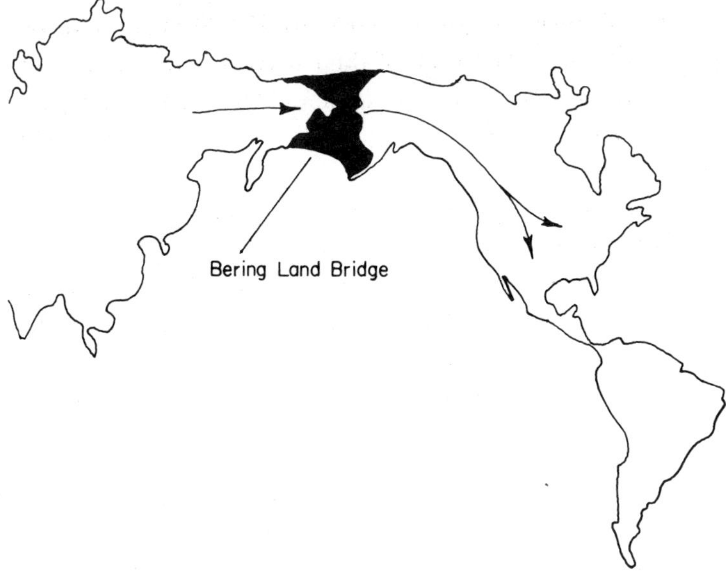

4-2 The Bering Land Bridge and the supposed route of Asian hunters into North America.

sea level dropped four hundred feet, it would result in the exposure of sea floor there at least seven hundred miles wide from north to south. This is certainly an area more than adequate to accommodate an influx of Arctic hunters and animals from Asia. Although this land was exposed at least four times during the past three million years, it appears that only during the later times was the opportunity to use it actually exploited. The now-inundated sea floor, when viewed as the conduit to the New World, is termed the Bering Land Bridge.

Once to the Alaskan interior, these early foragers dispensed to the south and east, eventually making it all the way to the southern tip of South America long before Columbus "discovered" the New World.

The use of the "bridge" by America's earliest human immigrants is supported not only by the geological findings but also by the work of physical anthropologists, those scientists who study modern human physical traits as well as the skeletal remains found in archaeological sites. Among the connections they have found between modern Native Americans and Asians are the similarities in blood types (both have A and O and lack B); the presence of the "Mongoloid spot" (a bluish patch of skin near the base of the spine on newborns); and shovel-shaped incisors, the condition in which the upper front teeth have a beveled-out appearance on their interior sides (actually enamel extensions built up on the tooth edges). No human remains have been found here that were anything other than modern in appearance, an indication of an in-migration after 35,000 B.P. or later.

It is not known when humans first set foot in the vicinity of the Black Hills. The best evidence places the event during Paleo-Indian times, slightly before 11,000 B.P. If people were there prior to that time, their track has so far remained concealed.

Clovis Foragers

Just to the east of the Black Hills, in a highly eroded region known as the Cheyenne–White River Badlands, a discovery of mammoth elephant bones was made by a Hot Springs avocational archaeologist, Les Ferguson. South Dakota archaeologist, Dr. Adrien Hannus of Augustana College, was informed of this find, and has spent four seasons there since 1980, excavating the remains of an adult and a juvenile mammoth.

In association with these butchered bones were three whole and fragmentary fluted spear points, known from mammoth kill sites elsewhere across the plains as Clovis points. The characteristics of Clovis points include lanceolate shape (long, thin), flutes on both basal faces (grooves that assist in socketing the point into a wooden foreshaft), and basal edges grinding (the intentional smoothing of the point's lower edges in order to reduce the chance of cutting the animal sinew fibers used to bind the point to the foreshaft). Hannus also found a large number of bone fragments that appeared to have been intentionally flaked and then used in the butchering.

This Lange/Ferguson site is the only known Clovis kill site in South Dakota. It has several attributes that fall within the typical pattern of Clovis sites outside of the state. First is the date. Clovis sites generally date around 11,200 B.P. The archaeologists have as yet found no charcoal at Lange/Ferguson, but in processing an organic layer *overlaying* the bones (and thus younger than the kill) they obtained a date of 10,670 ± 300 B.P. This means that the site is older than that, which fits known Clovis occupation elsewhere.

A second piece of the pattern is the location. Lange/Ferguson is situated in and around what was in those days a spring-fed pond. The early elephants would have been attracted to the water, and the hunters, knowing their be-

4-3 Mammoth bones exposed at the Lange/Ferguson kill site in the South Dakota Badlands. (S. Cassells)

havior, could wait in hiding until the animals got into the water and muck and their movements were drastically slowed. Since these Clovis people were on foot and had only a spear technology (bows and arrows came much later), they would have had to get fairly close to their quarry, a dangerous job, whatever the weapon. Therefore, the chance for success on the hunt would be greatly enhanced if the animals were bogged down.

Another trait of the Clovis hunters was the apparent selection of female and young elephants, rather than a more massive and aggressive bull. At Lange/Ferguson there is a juvenile and an adult.

A second bone locality has recently been discovered at the site, and so it appears that at least three mammoths were killed there, though probably not all at the same time. Given the extreme difficulty of bringing down even a single elephant, Lange/Ferguson, was probably used on several occasions as were most Clovis sites with several animals.

The bones there are not the result of a single mass kill but probably an accumulation over time.

Just to the west of the Black Hills in Wyoming's Powder River Basin is the Carter/Kerr-McGee site, excavated in 1976 and 1977 under the direction of Dr. George Frison of the University of Wyoming. It is a complex site with successive levels of occupation that cover several thousand years.

Most important to this discussion is the lowest zone. In it were a number of fluted Clovis points, along with several bone fragments, including one identified as a camel metatarsal (lower leg) that had a depressed fracture from a heavy blow. Much of the level has been eroded, and it is difficult to determine the actual use of the site (kill, camp?). At any rate, it does demonstrate Clovis presence on the west side of the Hills, as well as the use of Pleistocene camels in the Clovis diet.

There are no known Clovis sites within the Black Hills proper, but the potential for them is good, based on the evidence of Lange/Ferguson and Carter/Kerr-McGee, in addition to the known presence of mammoths in the region

4-4 Excavation units at the Carter/Kerr-McGee site. (George Frison)

(including the earlier paleontological Hot Springs Mammoth site in the southern Hills).

During 1984 a highly disintegrated portion of a mammoth tusk was discovered near Deerfield Reservoir (Castle Creek drainage), buried beneath about ten feet of sediment. No artifacts or other cultural associations were observed, but this site could eventually turn out to be a major find.

What we know about Clovis people in general, and in western South Dakota in particular, is fairly limited. Although Clovis artifacts are known as far east as Nova Scotia and as far south as Mexico, their camps and kill sites are rare, and when discovered, are limited in content.

We do not know what types of houses they lived in, although mammoth hunters of Siberia apparently had circular skin huts with mammoth bones piled on the outside. We don't know what they ate besides the meat of mammoths, bison, ground sloths, horses, and camels. It is assumed that they gathered roots, berries, and other edible plants, but as of yet, we lack firm evidence for this activity.

They were skilled flint knappers, fashioning the superb Clovis points, inventing the flute that remains its hallmark today. Such an attribute on spearpoints is unknown elsewhere in the world. They apparently had a bone technology as well, able to make and use bone implements for expedient butchering tools, as well as more sophisticated bevel-ended points, and in one case, even an eyebolt-shaped shaft wrench, the later two known from Montana and Arizona respectively.

Perhaps it is because North American mammoth hunters are similar enough in their lifestyle to the Pleistocene big game hunters of Europe and Asia that we have such fascination with them. To have been able to survive at the end of the North American Ice Age by hunting gigantic beasts, now long-extinct, took great skill and courage. Their life was not easy, nor was it simple. The stereotype of unsophisticated early cultures is not accurate. Our best guesses are that they held onto a rich cultural heritage of technologies, survival skills, and traditions that has allowed their genes to still be part of the modern Native Americans today.

Folsom Foragers

Just as the Clovis presence is elusive in the Black Hills, so is its successor, Folsom.

The hunters and gatherers of Folsom times (around 10,500 to 10,000 B.P.) are best known from the Lindenmeier site, a camp in northern Colorado, and from a number of kills in Wyoming, Colorado, and New Mexico.

The first discovery of Folsom points within a dense bed of extinct bison bones in the late 1920s near Folsom, New Mexico, marked the beginning of Paleo-Indian archaeology. People then realized that there has been a human presence in North America during the terminal Ice Age, quite a revelation for those days.

The Folsom point is quite a technological marvel, being produced through a precise series of steps that culminated with the removal of long thin channel flakes along both point faces. The flutes they produced prove the cultural ties with the Clovis people, but also demonstrate increasingly complicated as well as more refined flaking skills.

Some Folsom points reportedly have been found on the surface in the Black Hills. Unfortunately, these discoveries have been made by private collectors, and the supposed sites remain unreported and uninvestigated.

Adrien Hannus has recently examined a Folsom site near Lange/Ferguson in the Badlands, feeling that it may retain some good research potential. This will be the first such site professionally investigated in South Dakota.

A Folsom level at Carter/Kerr-McGee included Folsom points and stone manufacturing debris, a number of what

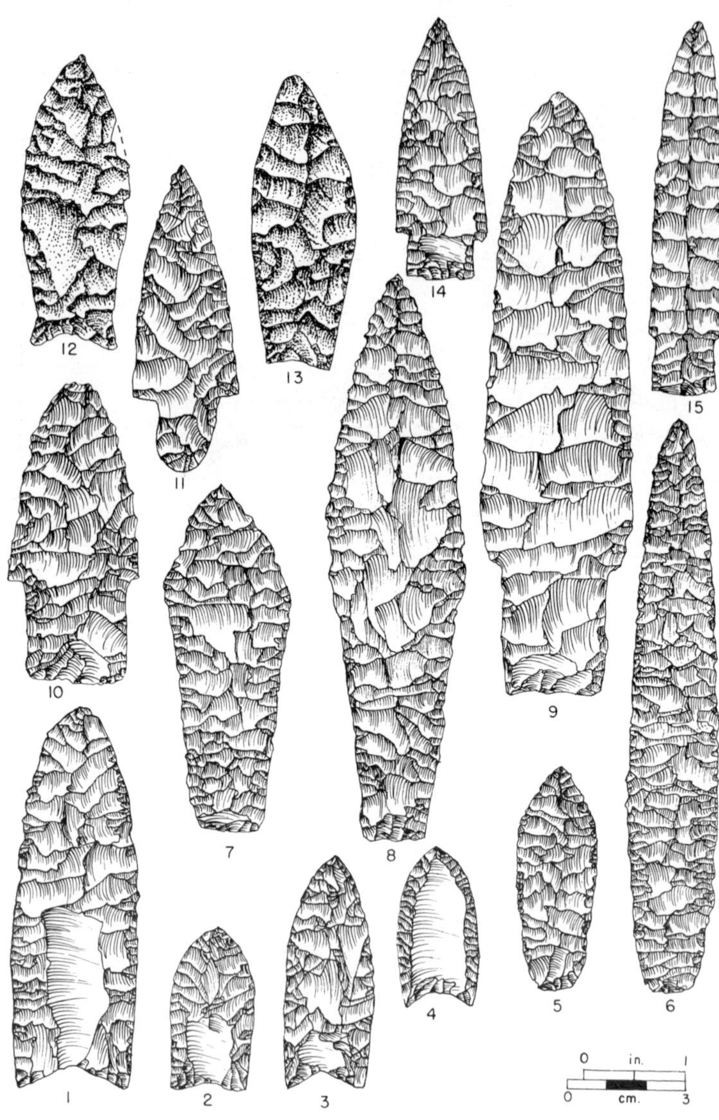

4-5 A sample of Paleo-Indian projectile points: 1-typical Clovis point; 2, 3- Clovis points from Lange/Ferguson; 4- typical Folsom point; 5- reworked Agate Basin point; 6- whole Agate Basin point; 7- reworked Hell Gap point; 8- whole Hell Gap point; 9- Alberta point from Hudson-Meng; 10- Alberta point from Trail Draw; 11- round base point like those from Andoni and Ditch Creek; 12- Lovell Constricted point from Andoni; 13- Angostura point from Ray Long; 14- typical Scottsbluff point (Cody Complex); 15- typical Eden point (Cody Complex).

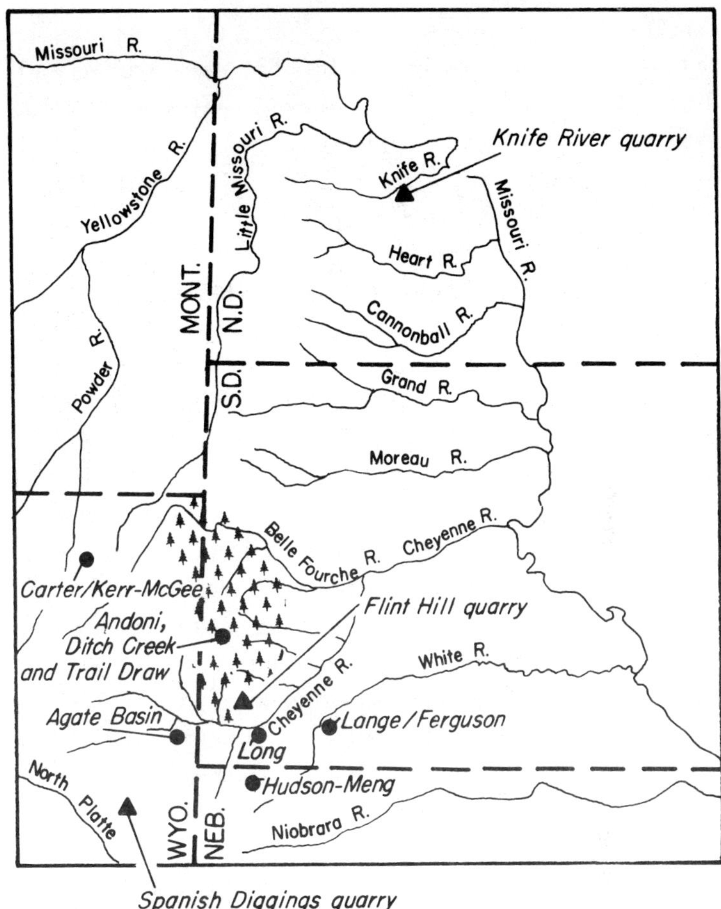

4-6 Map of Paleo-Indian sites and selected regional quarries.

appear to be bone and stone butchering tools, and a hearth. Charcoal from the hearth dated 10,400 ± 600 B.P. This Folsom component is probably a camp. Bison and mule deer appear to have been consumed by the occupants.

In terms of their lifeways, Folsom people were probably much the same as Clovis, with the exception that many of the Pleistocene big game were extinct by Folsom times. Most significant of those missing from the Folsom diet is the mammoth. Some scientists have speculated that human overkill was responsible for their demise, and it is probable that human hunting was a factor, but the warming and drying at the end of the Ice Age must have been even a greater influence on the extinctions.

Plano Foragers

With the fading of Folsom about 10,000 years ago, new stone tools began to appear. Fluting, a difficult practice that often resulted in breaking of the point during manufacture, was discontinued. Plano foragers appear to have existed in greater numbers than Folsom and Clovis people, because more of their sites are known around and in the Black Hills.

In 1946 archaeologists of the Missouri Basin Project (River Basin Surveys, Smithsonian Institution) came to the upper Cheyenne River where it coursed along the southern edge of the Black Hills. The impending construction of Angostura Reservoir there threatened untold archaeological sites, and federal funding was used to underwrite a systematic survey of the land that would be flooded. Among the sites discovered was the Ray Long site (39FA65). First work was begun there in 1948, and the excavators found a great deal of evidence for early human occupation along a terrace of the Cheyenne River. Buried beneath five to seven feet of soil was a zone that contained a number of hearths, along with camp related tools (scrapers, knives, perforators). Those types of artifacts tell us the function of such a site, but since the same styles of domestic tools can be found in many cultures covering at least ten thousand years, they do little to pin down a site in time or to give any distinctiveness to it.

However, projectile points often have identifiable styles, and some points were found, now termed Angostura points, that have been used as a cultural marker ever since. Angostura points, about three inches in length or slightly shorter,

4-7 Excavations at the Ray Long site in 1948. (R.P. Wheeler, Smithsonian Institution photo No. 49FA65-137)

are lanceolate in outline, generally have oblique flaking (flakes that trend at an angle across the blade faces, such as from upper left to lower right), and have the lower lateral edges ground smoothly, as with other Paleo-Indian points. The problem with the Angostura typology is that this point style has some stylistic overlap with three other types—Fredrick, Lusk, and Jimmy Allen—and thus is not as diagnostic as one might prefer. Some scholars lump these types into a category of oblique-flaked Plano points, leaving the specific name out. At the minimum, what this indicates is that the styles have more in common with each other than they do with Clovis, Folsom, or other more distinctive Plano points.

Surprisingly, the Long site contained a number of manos (handstones) and a grinding slab. Archaeologists have generally believed that the Paleo-Indians did not live solely on the meat of big game, but evidence from most sites has lacked proof of plant gathering and processing. Milling stones at Long, however, are direct evidence of plant processing and consumption and help to broaden our view of Paleo-Indian lifestyles.

The earliest date obtained from the Long site is 9,380 ±

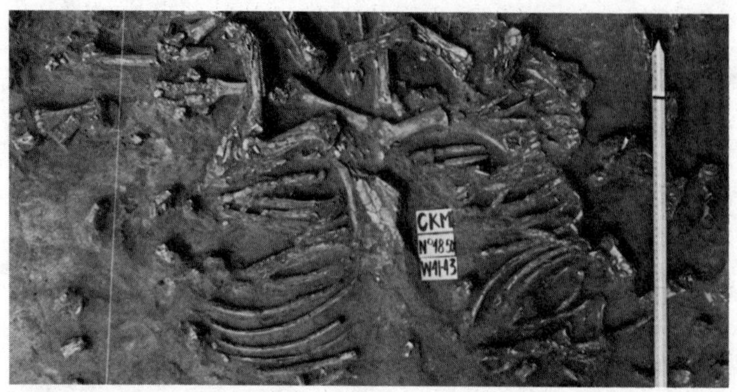

4-8 A portion of the bison bone bed in the Cody Complex zone (with Alberta, Eden, and Scottsbluff points) at Carter/Kerr-McGee. (George Frison)

500 B.P.. Two other samples, however, collected from what was thought to be the same zone although from outside the area with diagnostic artifacts, were dated at only 7,073 ± 300 B.P. and 7,715 ± 740 B.P.

Some Plano sites lie inside the Black Hills proper. Among them are the Andoni site (39PN326), just below the Limestone Plateau in the Central Area. A number of Lovell Constricted points were found on a disturbed surface, but no excavations have yet been undertaken. Lovell points, dating between 8,000 and 8,300 B.P., are best known from northern Wyoming. They have a broad blade with a contracting stem and a concave base. Grinding is found on both lateral base edges.

The Trail Draw site (39PN97), along the Limestone Plateau south of Deerfield Reservoir, yielded a single Alberta point as a surface find. Alberta points, broad-bladed and with a wide stem, are considered by many to fall within the Cody Complex with Scottsbluff and Eden points and Cody knives. The best reported Alberta site is Hudson-Meng, a bison kill in the Pine Ridge north of Crawford, Nebraska, that is dated between 8,900 ± 190 and 9,380 ± 100 B.P..

An Alberta component was also associated with Scottsbluff and Eden points at Carter/Kerr-McGee in Wyoming.

Interestingly enough, the raw stone material used to make the Alberta points at Hudson-Meng came from two major sources, the Knife River area in western North Dakota and the Flint Hills quarry in the southern Black Hills. This indicates widespread travel and/or trade during Paleo-Indian times.

One poorly known Paleo-Indian point type discovered in the Black Hills, at the Ditch Creek and Andoni sites, is a triangular bladed point with a narrow rounded stem. This type has been dated at the Medicine Lodge Creek site in the Bighorns at 9,590 ± 180 B.P. Some similarity exists between it and a point found at Lind Coulee in Washington state. At this time, no name has been applied to the style in Wyoming and South Dakota and little is known about its makers.

It is appropriate to note that there are a number of Plano point styles known from the plains that have not been found in the Black Hills, although the potential for such a discovery in the future is great. These styles include Hell Gap, Agate Basin, Scottsbluff, Eden, Pryor Stemmed, and Cody knives. Sites containing such styles are well known in Wyoming, Nebraska, and other surrounding states and include Agate Basin, Hell Gap, and Carter/Kerr-McGee in Wyoming, and Scottsbluff in Nebraska.

Summary

Paleo-Indians, as our continent's earliest inhabitants, were free-ranging nomads who employed a variety of skills to survive in a wild and challenging environment. The Black Hills, with abundant game and water, and numerous usable stone outcrops, were undoubtedly attractive to them. The mild southern Hills climate could have allowed groups to remain there during the harsh winter months, and the cooler

Interior and northern Hills would have been ideal for a hot summer refuge. Small hunting parties would probably disperse from larger base camps along permanent water and after obtaining their quarry would return to the main band.

There is no evidence in or around the Black Hills that Paleo-Indians lived in one place more than a short season. Instead, upon learning the terrain, the local vegetation distribution, and the game patterns, they could structure their seasonal movements to allow a fruitful return to the same haunts year after year.

References

On the Pleistocene and sea level fluctuations:
Müller-Beck 1967.
On the Bering Land Bridge:
Laughlin 1967; Müller-Beck 1967; Jennings 1968.
On Clovis culture:
Haynes 1974; Jennings 1968; Cassells 1983.
On the Lange/Ferguson site:
Hannus 1984.
On the Carter/Kerr-McGee site:
Frison 1984.
On Folsom culture:
Wilmsen and Roberts 1978; Jennings 1968; Cassells 1983.
On Plano culture.
Jennings 1968; Frison 1978; Cassells 1983; Agenbroad 1978.
On the Ray Long site:
Hughes 1949; Hughes and White n.d.
On the Andoni site:
Eckles 1978; Cassells, Miller, and Miller 1984.
On the Trail Draw site:
Tratebas 1978; Tratebas and Vagstad 1979; Cassells, Miller, and Miller 1984.
On the Ditch Creek site:
Tratebas 1976; Tratebas and Vagstad 1979; Cassells, Miller, and Miller 1984.

THE ARCHAIC 5

The sun had yet to come up over the horizon, and as Kwakal opened his eyes, he looked out past the edge of the overhang and could see the Pointed Rocks silhouetted on the eastern skyline. Ice hung heavily on the grasses this early fall morning, and Kwakal's breath filled the air like smoke from a green-wood fire.

Kwakal shook his brother's shoulder gently, rousing him from a deep sleep. They had a long trek in front of them and had to start early if they were to get back before dark. The band was about to move farther south, but Kwakal and his brother wanted to quarry stone one last time at a special rock outcrop on the plateau to the west.

Gathering their skins about their shoulders, they picked up their weapons, pushing extra foreshafts and points into their belts. Their thick elk-soled moccasins made little sound as they walked through the forest. The hunters were always on the alert for wild game of any kind.

The frost was gone and the warming sun was not quite overhead when they reached the white jagged cliffs with the flowing springs and bands of special stone that could be so easily made into strong spearpoints, knives, and scrapers. The two men laid down their atlatls and spears, searched around for a moment to locate a few stone cobbles, and then began smashing them against the wall of the rock outcrop.

Flakes and chunks were soon flying. Kwakal watched for a fissure to develop around a particularly nice piece of rock, and when it opened sufficiently, he took a sharpened branch and drove it in like a wedge and began prying. The combination of direct striking and prying soon loosened it, and it tumbled out onto the ground where Kwakal then drove off a series of large pink flakes.

After the two had set aside nearly 60 palm-sized flakes, they switched to smaller rounded river stones and used them to chip off the edges of the flakes, thinning and working them to a more oblong shape. It was not necessary to carry thick, heavy stone back to camp, only to flake away large quantities later while finishing each tool. The leaf-shaped bifaces they finally cached in their waist bags would function nicely as knives right now, and could later be turned into a number of other implements with a minimum of effort.

On the way back to camp, the hunters silently approached a large meadow. The long-needled pine gave way on the edge of the clearing to quaking aspen, their leaves now golden in the dying sunlight. Up ahead a herd of deer browsed on low bushes beneath the aspen.

Kwakal saw them first and motioned his brother down. The pair squatted in the underbrush for a few moments to let their excited hearts slow. Then each hunter grasped the fingerhold on his atlatl and seated the hook on the back end into the socket at the base of his feathered spearshaft. With their throwing hands steadying the shafts on the atlatls, they cocked their arms in preparation for launching the projectiles. A slight breeze came up over the hunters' backs, and the deer caught the scent. Their heads whirled toward the men, but their eyes could not see the two-legged predators. Kwakal knew their chances of success would

5-1 Two Archaic hunters release spears from their atlatls, hoping to bring down a deer in an aspen-ringed clearing. (Robin Farrington)

diminish if they hesitated much longer. With a mighty heave, he swung his arm forward and the long spear cut through the air, its shaft flexing as it flew. Then the other one was launched. Kwakal's missile flew over the back of a big buck and stuck in a tree with a loud whack. His brother's spear found its mark just behind the front leg of a fat doe. It was a perfect lung shot. The doe bolted but managed only a few steps before collapsing.

Kwakal patted his brother on the back and they both smiled. They watched the herd bounce off through the timber, and they waited patiently for the doe to cool and stiffen before approaching her. The fittest would survive another day.

When the Ice Age Left

For several thousand years Paleo-Indians moved throughout the Black Hills region with what appears to have been a focus on herds of large Pleistocene animals and wild plants. In time, these first Americans gained a solid foothold, increasing in number and density.

By about seven thousand years ago, in what is now termed the Archaic Stage, the effects of the post-Pleistocene climate on local inhabitants were significant. The large bison were either extinct or nearly so, being gradually replaced by modern *Bison bison.* With an increasingly warmer and drier environment, many wild plants presumably changed in frequency if they did not disappear altogether, while others became prominant in the available ecological niches.

The dramatically increased number of grinding implements (manos and metates) in Archaic sites seems to support the archaeological interpretation that the people of this time broadened the range of what they ate. Along with smaller modern bison and lesser game (deer, rabbits), a wide variety of plant food appears to have been added to their diet.

There were changes in their chipped-stone tool kits as well. The broad-stemmed and stemless Paleo-Indian points with ground basal edges were replaced by shorter notched and stemmed forms. Basal grinding was carried over, being employed by some flint knappers both inside the notches as well as on the bottom edge of the Archaic points. As viewed esthetically from our modern perspective, the quality of projectile point manufacturing overall began to go into a decline during the Archaic, a trend that was never to be reversed.

These Archaic projectiles were propelled by atlatls (throwing sticks), which acted as arm extenders and increased the velocity of the spears. There is limited evidence of some atlatl use during Paleo-Indian times, but during the Archaic it was beyond doubt a significant hunting weapon. The bow and arrow would not become part of the aboriginal arsenal until the Woodland Period, several millenia later.

The Altithermal

Interpretation of Archaic data, especially from the plains, has been influenced by the research and writing of Ernst Antevs. He published papers on former environments of the American West, proposing that the past 10,000 years be divided into three climatic episodes. The Anathermal, from 10,000 to 7,000 B.P., is thought to have been cooler and wetter than now. From around 7,000 to 4,500 B.P. was the Altithermal, a time drier and warmer than at present. Finally, the Medithermal, from about 4,500 B.P. up to current times, saw moisture increasing and temperature falling to present conditions. The Antevs model is based on evidence of erosional and depositional cycles, as seen in strata throughout the western United States. Of greatest interest to most archaeologists is the Altithermal, because in an area

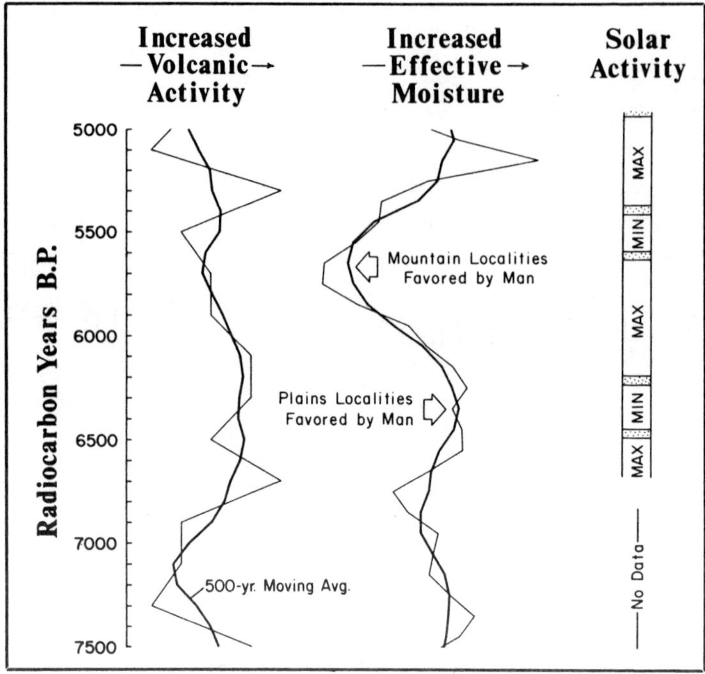

5-2 Correlation of volcanic activity, moisture changes, and solar activity during the Altithermal. (Benedict 1981)

like the plains that often seems to teeter on the brink of climatic disaster, a significant drying could dramatically alter the scope of life.

With the Altithermal concept in mind, archaeologists for years looked for evidence of human presence on the plains in the 7,500 to 4,500 B.P. range. They found little, and this seemed to confirm the Antevs hypothesis. With such adverse climatic conditions, Early Archaic hunter-gatherers would appear to have been forced to move to adjacent areas. William Mulloy, a pioneer Wyoming archaeologist, went so far as to term this time the "Altithermal Hiatus."

Colorado archaeologist/geologist James Benedict has conducted a great deal of research on this problem and believes that the Altithermal foragers sought out the higher altitudes as a refuge from the heat and desiccation. Benedict has derived population curves based on radiocarbon dates from known Altithermal sites in a large area of the western United States, Canada, and Mexico. He thinks that, based on these curves, there were probably two major Altithermal droughts, 7,000 to 6,500 B.P. and 6,000 to 5,500 B.P., separated by an interval of increased moisture and local mountain glaciation. This interval would have allowed a successful habitation of the lower peripheral plains, plateaus, and basins.

Benedict has found interesting correlations between decreased volcanic activity, decreased effective moisture, and increased solar activity during this time, the three combining as a possible explanation for the Altithermal.

If Benedict's "mountain refugium" model is true, and he does have good evidence from Colorado's alpine, then one might expect the Black Hills to also have a comparatively high number of Altithermal, or what are known as Early Archaic sites. In fact, a recent study has shown just the opposite. A forthcoming Ph.D. dissertation by Alice Tratebas on the archaeology of the Black Hills includes the statement that, "The present evidence shows the lightest use of the mountain uplift during the Altithermal."

In reality, the Black Hills case need not be seen as contradictory to the Benedict "mountain refugium" model. It should be noted that the Black Hills differ from the Rocky Mountains in that even in the cooler climate of today (as opposed to the Altithermal) the Black Hills do not retain permanent snowbanks. Benedict feels that it would take such a source of water during the Altithermal to lure a human population under stress from the dry plains. The Hills are not as dramatically different in altitude from the surrounding prairies as are the higher Rocky Mountains, and without snowbanks or glacial remnants might not have held sufficient moisture during the peak of desiccation to sustain a major influx of hunter-gatherers.

The Early Archaic: Hawken

Of the few Early Archaic sites known from the Black Hills, the most thoroughly investigated is Hawken, an arroyo bison trap on the western flank of the Hills south of Sundance, Wyoming. It was excavated during 1972 by George Frison of the University of Wyoming. In his reconstruction, the bison were driven at speed up the arroyo, a technique used to prevent them from turning around and escaping. Hunters were probably stationed along the route to keep the arrivals moving and to direct them up the correct fork of the arroyo. Once they reached its upper limits and were pinched off by the narrowing course, they were killed with spears. Nearly 300 projectile points were recovered at Hawken, along with the butchered remains of almost 100

5-3 View upslope along the gully used to trap the Hawken bison. (George Frison)

5-4 Excavation units at the Hawken site. (George Frison)

bison (scientifically classified as *Bison bison occidentalis*, an intermediate form between the Ice Age *Bison antiquus* and modern *Bison bison*). From tooth analysis Frison concludes that the site was the scene of one or more winter kills. The unusual number of bulls found indicates that at least one of the herds driven into the arroyo was all male, a composition typical of the season when bulls would not run with the cows and immature bison. Generally, however, bulls were not hunted, since nursery herds were probably easier to slaughter.

Radiocarbon dates from Hawken place it well within the Early Archaic at 6,470 ± 140 and 6,270 ± 170 B.P.. A nearby butchering area, named Hawken III, dates 6,010 ± 170 B.P.. In light of the discussion about the Black Hills' likely unsuitability during the Altithermal, it is interesting to note that these dates from the two Hawken localities place the site in Benedict's 6,500 to 6,000 B.P. interval when increased moisture allowed human dispersion to areas peripheral to mountain refugia.

The Middle Archaic: McKean

Bill Mulloy (1917-1978) put in over 25 years of archaeological work on the Northwestern Plains, principally in Wyoming and Montana, and is considered one of the region's most influential prehistorians. Of the many plains sites he investigated while on the faculty of the University of Wyoming, one of the better known is the McKean Site (48CK7).

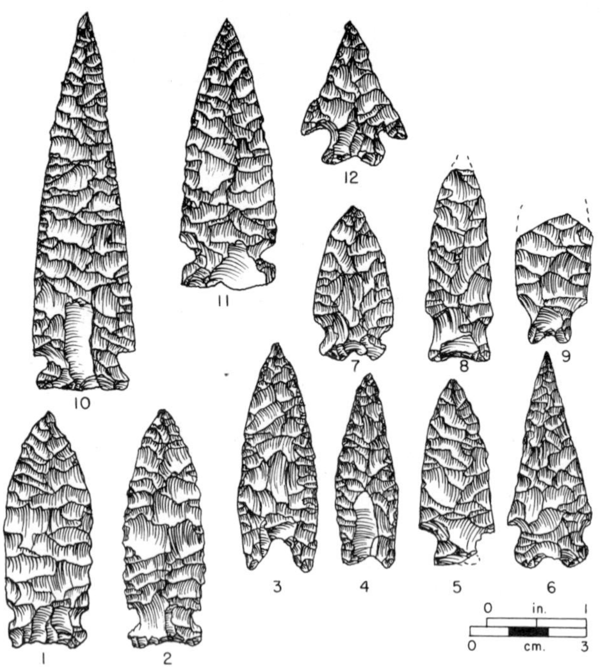

5-5 A sample of Archaic projectile points: 1, 2- Early Archaic points, Hawken; 3, 4- typical McKean Lanceolates; 5- Hanna point from George Hey; 6- Hanna variant; 7- Duncan variant; 8- Duncan point from George Hey; 9- Duncan variant from Twin Sisters; 10, 11- Besant points; 12- Pelican Lake point.

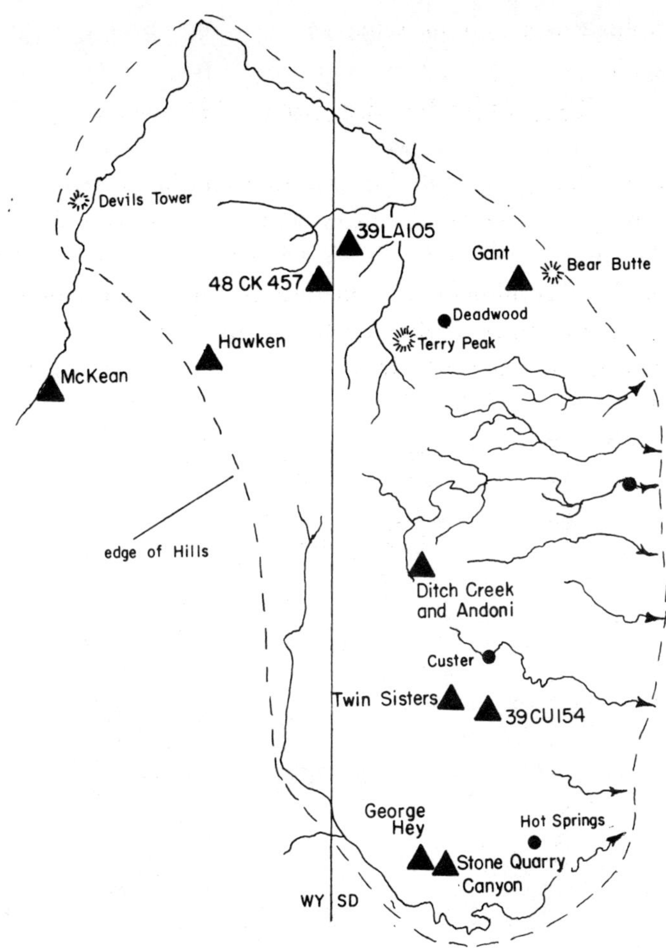

5-6 Map of selected Archaic sites in the Black Hills.

The Belle Fourche River valley on the Wyoming side of the Black Hills was going to be inundated by the construction of Keyhole Dam. Of sixty sites known within the maximum pool level, three were chosen by the University of Wyoming and the National Park Service to be excavated.

Under the direction of Mulloy, the McKean site was approached first, and the fieldwork during the 1951 and 1952 seasons was so productive that the other two sites were soon forgotten.

Two distinct levels were identified, each containing a dense concentration of fire hearths. The lower level also held a human cranium. Lanceolate and stemmed projectile points from the lower levels have since been named for this type site. The McKean Complex of tools includes McKean Lanceolate, Hanna, and Duncan points. A fourth type, found in some McKean sites (although not at Keyhole Reservoir), is the Mallory point; it has side notches and occasionally a deep basal notch. Notch, stem, and basal grinding, common on Early Archaic points, is typically missing on these Middle Archaic forms.

There has been some controversy about projectile point diversity during the Middle Archaic in this area. The significance of the occurance of the four McKean Complex types together is still being debated. Is it evidence of a periodic

5-7 Archaeologist exposing one of several fire hearths at the McKean type site in 1951-52. Note Mulloy's camp in the background. (University of Wyoming)

5-8 Bill Mulloy at the McKean site, 1951-52. (University of Wyoming)

gathering of diverse groups? Or are there undetected stratigraphic separations in sites that contain the different points, indicating differences in date and/or culture among the styles? Or does it point to a given Middle Archaic group using a variety of stylistic and/or functionally distinct projectile points at the same time? So far no explanation has been accepted by the archaeological community as a whole.

Dates for Middle Archaic McKean Complex sites range from about 3,000 to 5,000 B.P.. Although no C-14 dates were obtained from the lower level at the original McKean Site, a date of 3,287 ± 600 came from the upper post-McKean level there.

Trying to calculate population densities in the Black Hills is not practical yet. Our site record in the Hills is far from complete, and the variety of research strategies responsible for locating these sites could easily have skewed the results. However, because of the many McKean sites already found, it is tempting to suggest that Middle Archaic foragers made greater use of the Black Hills than those of any period before or since.

Archaeologist Alice Tratebas has concluded that McKean sites are more numerous than any other type in the Hills, and that they are the largest, suggesting that McKean foragers remained in place longer than other people. She found that of all McKean sites those at high discharge springs and along permanent creeks on the Limestone Plateau are the largest, probably indicating longer-term occupation than at smaller Central Core sites at low discharge springs. On the southern Hogback, Tratebas has recognized two site patterns. One includes primarily woodworking tools, which suggests a manufacturing site for spear shafts and other wooden implements. The other contains camp tools (grinding stones, scrapers, knives, hammerstones), hearths, and animal bones. This type of site is usually located at the base of a knoll or on a shelf below a series of higher ridges or knolls. These "protected" sites in the climatically mildest portion of the Black Hills are probably winter camps.

McKean sites in the Black Hills include Gant (39ME9) near the northern Hogback, Ditch Creek (39PN90) and the Andoni Site (39PN326) in the Limestone Plateau/Central Core contact area, Twin Sisters (39CU566) in the southern Central Core, and George Hey (39FA302) and one of the Stone Quarry Canyon sites (39FA396) on the Hogback of the southern Black Hills.

The Late Archaic

Following the people of the Middle Archaic were the hunters of the Late Archaic, whose lifeway was probably indistinguishable from that of their predecessors. The style of projectile points, however, is different. There are difficulties in defining point styles as in the Early Archaic. Elsewhere Besant and Pelican Lake points are major hallmarks of Late Archaic presence. In the Black Hills, however, neither of these types have been *absolutely* identified. Both

Besant points and the Early Archaic points from sites like Hawken are large side-notched forms, and there is at least some superficial stylistic overlap between them, making field identification difficult under the best of circumstances.

At 39CU154, a rockshelter found during the survey of the Mayo Timber Sale south of Custer, a large side-notched point *resembling* the Besant style was recovered. A reworked side-notched point of Knife River Flint (from North Dakota) was found during a survey northwest of Tinton in the northern Hills at site 48CK457. Its notches were heavily ground, a trait of the period.

Large corner-notched points, perhaps related to Pelican Lake, have been found at several sites, such as 39LA105. Alice Tratebas found a significant correlation between keeled (oblong, high backed) scrapers and these points, and she suspects that the scrapers may have been used in preparing shafts and other woodworking. She also believes that the Late Archaic foragers used the Central Core more than most other groups, excluding McKean.

In the region as a whole, the Late Archaic probably lasted from about 3,000 to 1,500 B.P. (until around A.D. 500). However, more accurate generalizations about the Late Archaic in the Black Hills will have to wait for the accumulation of a solid range of dates from sites that have good associations with Late Archaic diagnostic artifacts.

Summary

The Archaic appears to have been the longest period maintained in the New World. (It is understood, of course, that the Archaic, like other periods, is an artificial construction by modern archaeologists.) For 7,000 years or more, post-Pleistocene Archaic foragers moved about, exploiting a wide variety of ecological niches, claiming as their own a drier and warmer land than that held by their Siberian ancestors. The adjustments required in the face of environmental change were obviously met, and the cultures survived.

We may never know all of the trials these people endured nor all of their innovations. We cannot know how they regarded these Black Hills. Were they sacred? Were they a sanctuary from the blast furnace winds of the Altithermal?

By the beginning of the Christian Era, the western prairie began to witness a new way of life. New influences were filtering north and west up the Missouri River, and it was only a matter of time before the Black Hills were touched.

References

On the Archaic:

Jennings 1968; Frison 1978; Cassells 1983.

On the Altithermal:

Antevs 1948, 1955; Martin and Mehringer 1965; Bryson, Baerreis, and Wendlund 1970; Bryan and Gruhn 1964; Benedict 1979, 1981.

On the Hawken site:

Frison 1978; Frison et al. 1976.

On McKean and the Middle Archaic:

Mulloy 1954; Wheeler 1952, 1954; Frison 1978; Tratebas n.d.

On the Gant site:

Gant and Hurt 1965.

On the Twin Sisters site:

Cassells 1981.

On the George Hey site:

Tratebas and Vagstad 1979.

On the Stone Quarry Canyon sites:

Tratebas 1979.

On Besant, Pelican Lake, and the Late Archaic:

Tratebas n.d.; Frison 1978; Cassells, Miller, and Miller 1984; Wettlaufer 1955; Wettlaufer and Mayer-Oakes 1960.

On 39CU154 site:
Groenfeldt 1978.
On 48CK457 site:
Cassells 1982.
On 39LA105 site:
Tratebas 1978.
On the correlation of keeled scrapers with Late Archaic points:
Tratebas n.d.

6-1 A variety of domestic tasks are being performed in this camp of Woodland people. (Left to right) A women grinds seeds with the aid of a mano and grinding slab, another is working with a fresh hide from a deer, while a third is shaping a ceramic vessel by paddling the exterior with a cord-wrapped stick. In the background, a mother converses with her child. To the right one man is detaching flakes from a core by indirect percussion (hammerstone to antler tine to core), and the other flintnapper is finishing a tool by fine pressure flaking with an antler tip. Skin covered huts, encircled with stones, serve as shelters. The exterior cooking hearth suggests a warm season.

THE POST-ARCHAIC 6

With the coming dawn a gray light filtered into the rock shelter. Deer skins hanging across the entrance could neither keep out the sun nor hold in any warmth. A three-day spring blizzard had pounded the high prairie, laying a broad white blanket on the land and driving every living creature into some form of refuge. Haida and his family were fortunate. They knew of this little south-facing cave in the Hogback and had run there when the sky signs were unmistakable, long before the first blast slammed into the tan sandstone walls of the ridge and bent pine trees to the ground.

Haida kept the bison robe over his back as he pulled the doorway skin to one side and peered out. Endless drifts stretched out like white snakes, their unseen heads lying somewhere over the southern horizon, far beyond the Cheyenne River terraces and near the Pine Ridge cliffs, a three-day walk away.

"What is it, father? What do you see?" a small boy asked from the depths of his sleeping robe.

"The storm is past, son. The day will be cold but clear. Can you hear the silence? The wind has gone east chasing the snow."

"Do we move today?"

"No," replied Haida, "the snow is too deep. We still have plenty of food from the deer your brother killed. With that and some of last fall's pemmican, we will feast as we did at the Sun Dance. Our bellies will cry out for fear of bursting. We do not need to move yet." Haida crawled back near the rest of the family and snuggled in, the warmth of his wife and two sons flooding over him.

Later, when the sun was high, Haida's wife built a fire in the cave mouth and roasted venison over the coals. The hides had been drawn back, and black smoke trailed upward into the cloudless sky. The fire sign did not go unnoticed. Before evening visitors approached.

"Ha! May we enter?" came a cry from outside.

Haida quickly grasped a spear, motioned his family to the rear of the cave, and stood up. He knew his muscular frame was intimidating and he used it to its full advantage. "Ha!" he said. "Who are you and what do you want?"

A frail man, gray hair at his temples, stepped forward from a ragged group of two women and a child. "I am Chalang of the Beaver People. We have been here in the Black Hills country for only a short time. We walked west along the Cheyenne River from our hunting grounds around the Big Muddy. Three days ago we were caught by the storm without any protection. My son went searching for better shelter and did not return. We fear he is dead now. We are without any food and are very cold."

Haida thought first of his family and then of his ample meat cache. If he were killed in a storm, he hoped someone would take in his wife and children. "Enter, friends. We have food and many robes. Our camp is yours."

The travelers from the east ate well and slept soundly that night, recovering from the exhaustion of the previous days. The next day they sat around the warming fire exchanging stories of strange places visited and adventures long past.

The following morning they could see that the snow was thinning in places, and along the base of the southern Hogback heat radiating from the rocks had completely cleared the ground. The old man and his family were anxious to move back to the Big Muddy River, and they made preparations to leave. Without their main hunter, it made little sense to stay on in the Black Hills. They needed the security of the other Beaver People.

"Thank you, Haida. Thanks to all of you for what you've done. Your warmth is like that of Mother Sun, and your generosity is greater than Father Earth when he sends the ducks and geese in the fall. We shall not forget you. Our hearth is always open to you and all your people. Farewell." Chalang waved and turned to the opening.

His wife motioned with a gnarled finger. Her smile was wide, exposing a mouth nearly vacant of teeth. She reached into a bundle suspended from her shoulder and extracted a small cone-shaped pottery vessel. Holding it out with both hands to Haida's wife, she nodded several times, encouraging its acceptance. When it was taken, the Beaver woman clapped her hands with excitement. "Yours," she said gleefully and disappeared after her band.

Haida's wife hefted the small jar in her hands. It was heavy for its size. She ran her hands over its exterior. It was rough. When she looked at it in the light she saw lines like twisted cords pushed into the surface. She slid her hands around the inside. It was polished smooth.

"What is it?" asked Haida.

"Some sort of stone basket."

"Does a person make such a thing?"

"I do not know," she said. "Perhaps it floats down their Big Muddy from the north. Whatever, I know that I will treasure this. We may never see another."

The pot was passed carefully around the family, and they marvelled at its symmetry and hardness.

Haida's wife looked out to the east and watched as the Beaver People slowly disappeared around the rocks. She mulled over in her mind the encounter with these visitors from another world and the gift they left behind.

Cultural and Scientific Overlap

The Black Hills are a middle ground. Situated on the border of Wyoming and South Dakota, they lie between two prehistoric culture areas, the Northwestern Plains and the Middle Missouri. Not only did prehistoric groups from both areas frequent the Hills, probably making cross-cultural contact and perhaps sharing new ideas, but in more recent times, archaeologists from both areas have also penetrated the region. Analytical complications have resulted.

During Paleo-Indian and Archaic times, little distinguishes Northwestern Plains and Middle Missouri dwellers, but the post-Archaic is another matter. Sometime after A.D. 1, stratified societies from the Eastern Woodlands spread their influence westward, and the results were the development of a number of ceramic-producing, sedentary, horticultural groups living in eastern South Dakota and along the Missouri Trench. These people were to dominate that region for the next 1,700 years.

To the west, however, life continued much the same as during the preceding Archaic, save for the adoption of the bow and arrow around A.D. 500. The aboriginals continued to hunt wild game and to gather wild plant foods and materials while moving about in the nomadic patterns common on the dry western prairies for millennia.

Archaeologists who work with the distinctive ceramic and architectural traits associated with Middle Missouri cultures do not hesitate to classify Black Hills ceramic sites as part of the well-established Middle Missouri taxonomy. Northwestern Plains archaeologists, generally using the less complex taxonomy of post-Archaic hunter-gatherers, lump them into a post-A.D. 500 period known as the Late Prehistoric.

Once a person understands that the Black Hills were the domain of different but contemporaneous post-Archaic cultures and that at least two archaeological taxonomies have been applied to the groups of the region, there is less chance of confusion when reading current archaeological literature.

The Late Prehistoric: Vore

The break between the Late Archaic and the Late Prehistoric came with the introduction of the bow and arrow around A.D. 500. It is doubtful that the lifestyle changed here much. The Late Prehistoric bands relied on wild game and wild plants for subsistence, moving periodically in search of food and other resources. Until the horse was acquired during the 1700s, these foragers were pedestrians.

Bison hunting appears to have been a central focus for the Late Prehistoric people. A common technique was to force bison over a cliff, disabling the animals so that they could be shot with arrows and killed. The Northwestern Plains have a large number of these sites, with the greatest concentration being from Wyoming north into Canada. Hunters often herded the bison by driving them along rock alignments and lines of other hunters on a predetermined course of up to a mile or more to the jump-off point. This operation required considerable coordination and cooperation between hunters and would probably have involved several bands joined together for periodic communal drives.

One of the more interesting remnants of bison hunting is a site in the Black Hills known as the Vore site, located in the Red Valley between Sundance and Beulah, Wyoming. The site, in a deep sinkhole, was discovered in 1970 and excavated over the next two seasons.

6-2 Two levels of bison bone in the Vore site as seen in the exposed walls of an excavation unit. (George Frison)

The sinkhole (a karst feature similar to the one at the Hot Springs mammoth site discussed in Chapter 3) is a relatively restricted target for a lengthy game drive, being only 30 meters in diameter. Its presence in the valley is not easily seen from any great distance, so the moving bison would not be alerted to danger until it was too late. The steep-sided walls and the depth of 17 meters would be more than adequate to disable the beasts.

Exposed at the site were up to 22 separate levels of bison bones, all apparently deposited between A.D. 1500 and 1800. It is likely that the later groups using the jump were mounted on horses.

The majority of artifacts with the bones were side-notched projectile points, some with basal notching as well. Butchering tools of both stone and bone were also recovered in the various levels.

An analysis of the raw materials used by the Vore hunters indicates that they quarried stone at local Black Hills sites and at other sites considerable distances away. Quartzites came from Spanish Diggings, west of Lusk, Wyoming, in

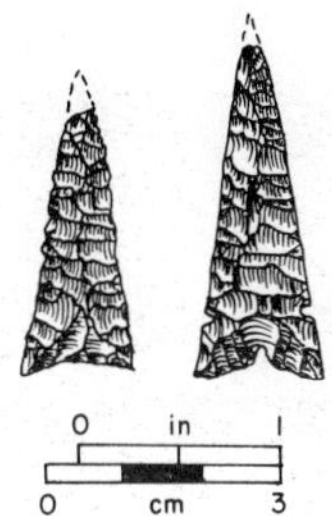

6-3 Two projectile points from the Vore site; (left) triangular; (right) side and basal notched.

the Hartville Uplift. Porcellanite is found to the west and north along the Powder and Tongue Rivers. Both of these sources are about 100 miles away. The third is 300 to 350 miles to the north, where a high quality brown chalcedony, Knife River Flint, was quarried.

A sample of mandibles (lower jaws) excavated at Vore has allowed archaeologists to estimate that over 10,000 and perhaps up to 20,000 bison were killed at the site during a 300 year period. The bones lie about five meters deep. After analyzing the mandibles to determine the ages of the animals at death, the investigators believe that kills took place throughout the year, beginning in late fall and extending into the spring and summer.

Vore is primarily a kill site and does not reveal anything about Late Prehistoric camping patterns. However, the circular arrangement of 40 to 50 bison skulls in one level hints at ceremonial practices.

Although Vore cannot be seen as typical, it does provide ample evidence of hunting efficiency during the Late Prehistoric.

The Plains Woodland

Significant regional distinctions appeared during post-Archaic times as traits from the eastern Woodlands began to infiltrate the plains. Because there is no real evidence for an in-migration of Hopewell peoples (the Middle Woodland

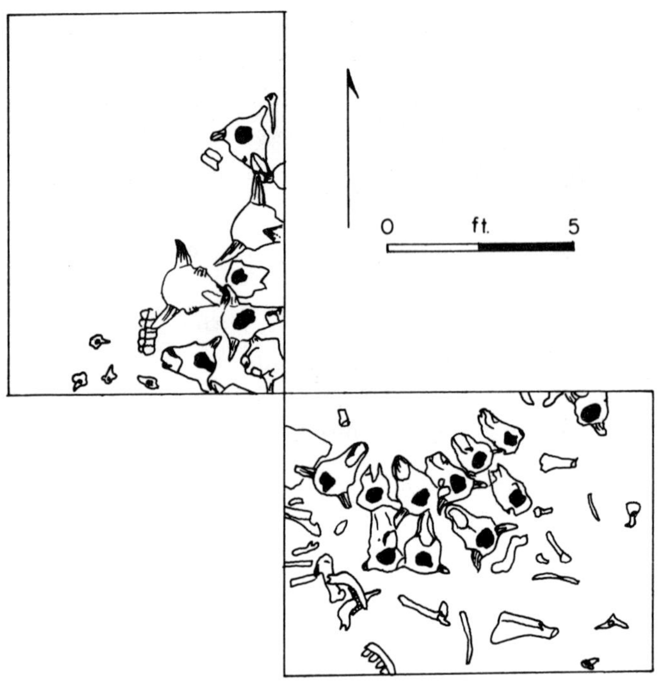

6-4 Plan of two Vore excavation units with exposed segments of a circle of bison skulls. The black areas on the foreheads indicate breakage for brain extraction during butchering.

culture of Illinois and the core of Woodland society), it is suspected that trade from the eastern nucleus into the plains was responsible for the transfer of new ideas. Thus cultural change was very likely brought about by diffusion, a latent function of economic pursuits.

The original Woodland of the Ohio, Illinois, and Mississippi valleys was highly advanced both technologically and socially. Archaeologial research points to a horticulturally-based and socially stratified population with widespread trade connections. There is no indication that the recipient Plains Woodland adopted the entire exotic culture. Instead, there are forms of a few significant Eastern qualities (such as semi-sedentism, cord-marked pottery, and burial mounds) in plains states. As might be expected from diffusion, the quantity of adopted traits declines with distance from the core area. The Plains Woodland of South Dakota can be seen as a somewhat degenerated version of the Eastern type, but can also be viewed as having its own identity.

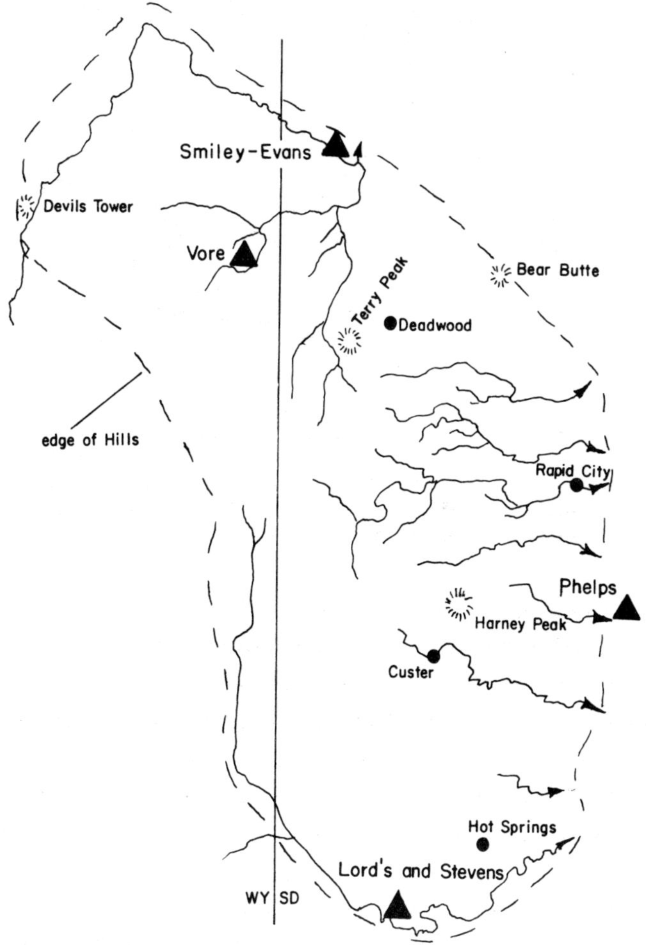

6-5 Map of selected Late Prehistoric, Plains Woodland, and Plains Village sites.

The first evidence of Woodland society in South Dakota appears about A.D. 1 near the southern state boundary along the Missouri River. It is called the Loseke Creek Complex of the Plains Woodland Period and is best seen in the Scalp Creek and Ellis Creek sites. Found at these sites were conical and rounded pottery with cord-roughened or cord-marked exteriors, side-notched projectile points, storage pits, and burial mounds. These sites appear to have been used until about A.D. 800.

Another group, the Sonota Complex, lived farther north on the Missouri. Much of our knowledge about them comes from burial mounds. Principal sites include Boundary Mounds, Grover Hand, Stelzer, Arpan, and Swift Bird. No horticultural evidence has been found with the mounds, but buffalo hunting on a large scale is assumed because of the large amounts of bone present. The Loseke Creek burials were mostly primary: the individuals were buried shortly after death and were never disturbed. The Sonota Complex burials, however, were usually secondary: the bodies in the graves had been previously buried in other graves or had been allowed to decompose somewhat before burial, perhaps in trees or scaffolds. Sonota Complex houses tended to be circular, and conical pottery (cord-marked or plain) was a probable late addition to their culture. Raw material for stone tools included local cherts from gravels, in addition to Knife River Flint from North Dakota and obsidian from Yellowstone. It is quite possible that these materials were used in trade with the Hopewell groups to the east.

The third Woodland type identified in South Dakota, the Dakota Mound Complex, is known primarily from the Sisseton Mound excavation in the northeastern part of the state. Large quantities of bison remains there may reflect affinities with the Sonota Complex farther west. Dakota Mound sites may date as late as A.D. 1150.

Some confusion between possible Woodland sites and

6-6 Excavations at the Lord's Ranch rockshelter group in 1939. (South Dakota Archaeological Research Center)

other cultures may occur in eastern South Dakota. Catlinite pipes and birchbark have been found in newer mounds, but they are probably either Assiniboin or Sioux in origin.

Woodland culture is not very well represented in the Black Hills. The first excavations to uncover Woodland evidence there were in two clusters of rockshelters that had been discovered originally by W.H. Over. In 1939, as part of a W.P.A. project, the Stevens Ranch and the Lord's Ranch rockshelter groups were examined under the direction of local enthusiast, Rev. James J. Pruitt, Jr., of Edgemont. As in many parts of the country, pothunters had beaten the investigators to the overhangs and had caused considerable disturbance. In addition to noting the previously turned soil, Rev. Pruitt also mentioned vandalism to rock art, both modern initials carved over prehistoric depictions and the hammering off of souvenirs.

Although the recovered artifacts from these two site clusters were relatively few, of special interest to the present discussion was the discovery of a number of cord-marked pottery sherds that indicated Plains Woodland presence in the southern Hills. Along with the ceramics were some small side-notched and corner-notched projectile points.

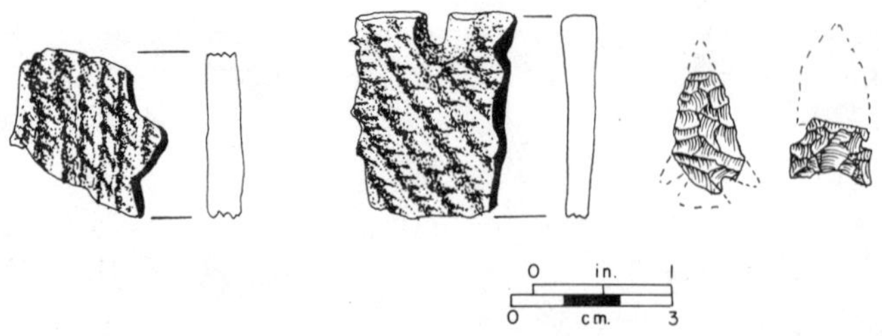

6-7 Two cord-marked pottery sherds and two small projectile points from Plains Woodland sites, the Stevens Ranch rockshelters.

Although sparse, there have been other discoveries of Woodland artifacts in the Black Hills—sufficient to confirm that the Plains Woodland extended west out of the major riverine systems more generally associated with them. In all likelihood, Woodland peoples in the Black Hills duplicated the lifeway of the Late Prehistoric foragers of the west, hunting and gathering wild resources, not settling in any one place or raising corn, beans, or squash. Very probably the Plains Woodland villages of the Missouri River area would send hunting parties out to the Black Hills and other places, with the idea that they would return with food and materials valuable to the larger group.

The Plains Village Pattern

About A.D. 800 a climatic episode known as the Neo-Atlantic began which brought more rainfall and a lower average temperature. This provided a better climate for crop production, and what followed has been termed the Plains Village Pattern or Tradition. Like the Plains Woodland, this culture on the plains was a diminished (or at least different) form of the eastern prototype. The nuclear area, Cahokia (near modern St. Louis), held a massive number of people, all practicing a complex culture known now as Mississippian. They were socially stratified and were highly dependent upon domesticated crops such as corn, beans, and squash. Their influence spread along the primary waterways, entering the plains via the Missouri River, although there is also some evidence for overland connections across Iowa and Minnesota.

Since evidence for Plains Villagers in the Black Hills is somewhat limited, the intricacies known from the Missouri Trench will be glossed over somewhat in the following discussion. Suffice it to say that from about A.D. 900 until Euro-American contact in the 1700s, the Missouri Trench was the scene of considerable cultural development and interaction.

Early horticulturalists of the Middle Missouri Tradition were the first of the Mississippian-influenced societies in the Trench, beginning around A.D. 900. They were joined about A.D. 1200 by offshoots of the Central Plains Tradition from eastern Nebraska and are known as the Coalescent Tradition in South Dakota. Slightly later the Oneota arrived in the Basin, probably from Iowa. Archaeologists have broken down taxonomically both the Middle Missouri and the Coalescent Traditions into a number of variants. A number of excellent references are available for those interested in pursuing this topic further.

The Middle Missouri Tradition

The influence of the Mississippian culture extended widely from the nuclear area around St. Louis. Flat-topped earthen temple mounds often characterize the villages and cities of the east and southeast. Fortifications surrounding many of these settlements suggest that the intrusion of this culture was not welcomed by all those who preceded the Mississippians.

In South Dakota the evidence concerning the sources of culture change from Woodland to Mississippian patterns is not clear-cut. It is difficult here, as in most archaeological

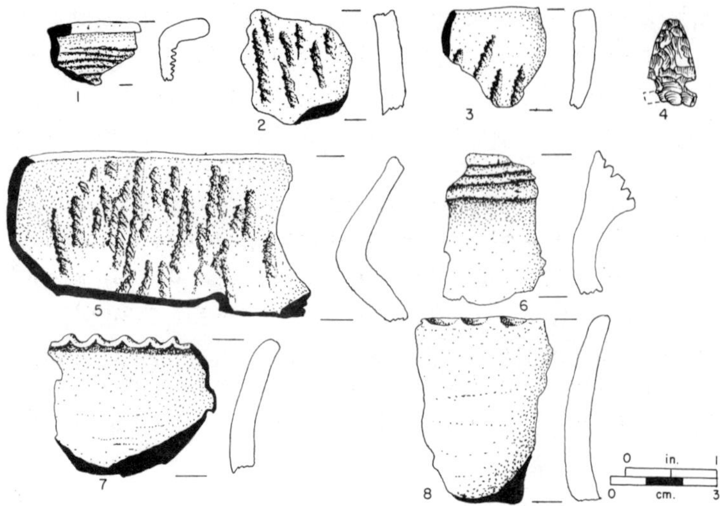

6-8 Middle Missouri Tradition artifacts from the Black Hills: 1, 2, 3- pottery sherds from Smiley-Evans; 4- projectile point from Smiley-Evans; 5, 6, 7, 8- pottery sherds from the Phelps site.

settings, to distinguish between what was an actual in-migration of people and what might have been only a heavy influence on local societies. At present the archaeological community is divided, and in fact it may be that what we see in the development of Middle Missouri villagers is a combination of both.

Most of the early villages (known as Initial Middle Missouri Variant) were no larger than 20 to 30 houses, although some, like the Goering site near Mitchell, S.D., held up to 90 or so of the square or rectangular semi-subterranean earth lodges, often enclosed by deep, steep-sided fortification ditches. Poles were placed inside the ditch to form a protective stockade line.

In the late 1950s a site was discovered by Bob Gant on a high, flat-topped spur overlooking the Belle Fourche River in the northern Black Hills. Named the Smiley-Evans site (39BU2), it now appears to be the westernmost example of Initial Middle Missouri Variant culture.

Excavations of the site by archaeologists Lynn and Bob Alex and the Northern Hills Chapter of the South Dakota Archaeological Society began in 1979. Dated A.D. 900 ± 70, it contains a number of elements common to Initial Middle Missouri sites along the Missouri River and farther east. These include a fortification ditch four to five meters wide, a line of posts inside the ditch, (probably a stockade wall), storage pits, small side-notched projectile points, and pottery sherds with cord-marking and some examples of out-flared rims with incised lines.

At present, many questions remain to be answered about Smiley-Evans. There is little evidence for farming at the site. Were the inhabitants a small group of Missouri River villagers who relocated to the west, or were they a local band who maintained contact with the east and adopted a few of their traits? The site has been only partially excavated, and it is possible that these and other questions can be answered in the future.

Another interesting occurence of off-river Plains Villagers is the Phelps site (39CU206), located east of the Hills near Hermosa. The site was exposed in 1930 by Mr. and Mrs. Walter Phelps when they were digging a basement near Battle Creek. Sherds found there resemble Initial Middle Missouri types. Trade goods include dentalium from the Pacific Ocean, conch shells from the Gulf Coast, and obsidian, perhaps from Wyoming. The large collection has since been donated to the South Dakota Archaeological Research Center in Ft. Meade.

A number of questions arise about the nature of the Phelps site inhabitants. Whether they were sojourners from the Mississippi or locals with a number of trade connections cannot be determined. Unfortunately there is little chance that anything is left at the site that could shed further light on the problem.

That both of these Initial Middle Missouri sites have

been discovered along the margins of the Black Hills proves that Middle Missouri villagers pushed west somewhat and that there is potential for similar discoveries in the Black Hills in the future.

At present there is no evidence for subsequent Missouri River groups in the Black Hills from A.D. 1400 to 1700. Since the Initial Middle Missouri peoples appear to have known of the Black Hills, there is little reason to believe that later groups did not also. However, if subsequent Missouri River cultures only hunted in the Hills for brief periods, the chances that archaeologists could distinguish their sites from local hunters is very remote.

Summary

The post-Archaic of the Black Hills is marked by the presence of several distinctive groups—the early Plains Woodland, the subsequent sedentary Plains Villagers, and the more westerly, mobile foragers of the Late Prehistoric.

It was a time of innovation when cultures met, joined, changed, and/or conflicted.

With hindsight we can see that although it must have seemed tumultuous at times to the people then, it was nothing compared to what was to come later when European civilization intruded into the land, shutting forever the door of "primitive" society on the plains.

References

On Late Prehistoric terminology:
Mulloy 1958; Frison 1978.
On Missouri River terminology:
Lehmer 1971; Zimmerman 1985.
On the Vore site:
Frison 1978; Reher and Frison 1980.
On the Plains Woodland:
Wedel 1961.

On the Loseke Creek Complex:
Hurt 1952.
On the Sonota Complex:
Neuman 1975.
On the Dakota Mound Complex:
Sigstad and Sigstad 1973.
On the Stevens Ranch and Lord's Ranch rockshelters:
Meleen and Pruitt, Jr. 1941.
On the Neo-Atlantic climatic pattern:
Baerris and Bryson 1965.
On the Mississippian nuclear area:
Moorehead 1928; Jennings 1968.
On the Plains Village Pattern along the Missouri River:
Lehmer 1971; Zimmerman 1985.
On the Smiley-Evans site:
L. Alex 1979; R. Alex 1981.
On the Phelps site:
Alex and Zimmerman 1979.

7-1 W.H. Over (right) and H.E. Lee camping in Red Canyon during their first expedition to the Black Hills, August 1925. (W.H. Over State Museum)

BLACK HILLS ROCK ART
7

The earliest archaeological work in the Black Hills was directed at the edges rather than the interior, and the first of those investigators was W.H. Over, Director of the University of South Dakota Museum in Vermillion from 1913 to 1949. A leading figure in South Dakota archaeology, Over's work centered on the village cultures in the eastern half of the state, but beginning in 1925 he also came to the Black Hills. There, in addition to identifying and recording a number of rockshelter groups and the now-famous Flint Hill quartzite quarry in the southern Hills, by the 1930s he discovered and reported several rock art panels around the margins of the Hills.

Then, during the Angostura Reservoir surveys and excavations between 1946 and 1950, other southern Hills rock art sites were discovered, and it became more obvious to the outside world that the Black Hills were a repository of prehistoric creative efforts painted, pecked, and carved on its vertical stone walls.

It was not until 1980, however, that the greatest contribution was made to our knowledge of Black Hills rock art. An intensive survey of the southern Hills was undertaken by Project Director Linea Sundstrom of the Archaeology Lab-

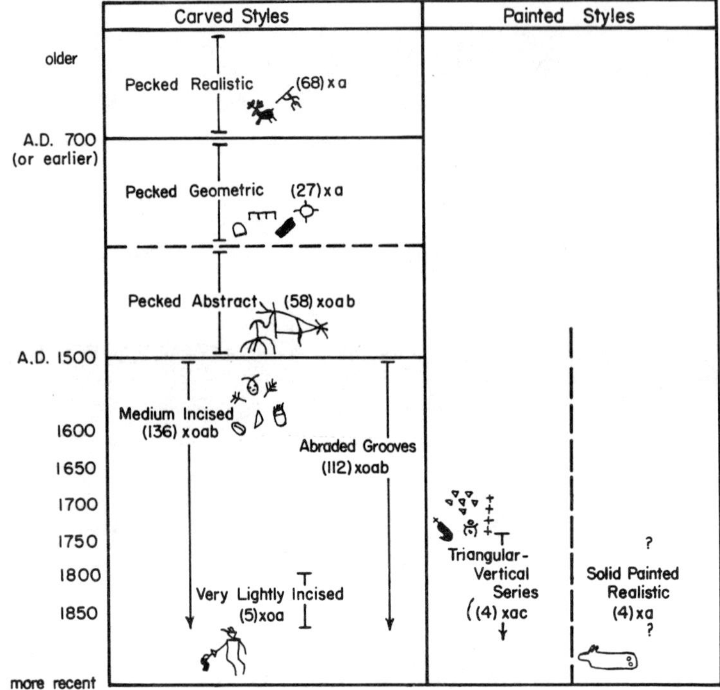

7-2 Proposed rock art sequence for the southern Black Hills. Time intervals *do not* represent the *span* of time for each style but indicate that each style falls somewhere between the two dates (modified from Sundstrom 1984, South Dakota Archaeological Society)

oratory, South Dakota State University, bringing the total of known and recorded southern Black Hills rock art sites to 69.

Sundstrom was able to sort out various panels into a chronological sequence by using five criteria. *Superposition*: one style of art has been executed over the top of another, indicating the relative age of each. *Relative weathering* and *relative patination of carvings*: more heavily weathered or patinated art at a site is assumed to be older than others less affected at the same site. *Relative age of panel surface*: art on newer surfaces (with more recent spalling) is probably younger than art on old, non-spalled surfaces at the same site. *Sediment displacement*: a judgement is made about the relative sediment deposition at the base of the panel, indicating that glyphs higher or lower on the wall may be older or younger in relation to each other; in other words, where was the ground level at the time the artist stood on it to produce the art? *Subject matter*: for example, bows and arrows rather than atlatls would indicate Late Prehistoric, Woodland or post-Woodland rather than Archaic or earlier. Painted panels were not included in these criteria but instead were compared to ethnographically recorded Indian art in other parts of the plains.

Overall, southern Black Hills rock art includes realistic forms during the earliest times and increasingly abstract styles later. During the Late Prehistoric, incised rock art returns to realism.

Sundstrom sees the Pecked Realistic as the earliest form, with subjects including a variety of animals. Humans are usually depicted in hunting scenes, often with atlatls or

7-3 Pecked Realistic rock art from 39FA94. (Linea Sundstrom)

7-4 Incised rock art from 39FA7. (Lindea Sundstrom)

spears. Stylistically, the work is most similar to art from Wyoming, Nevada, and California. Sundstrom's chronology places the style from 2500 B.C. or earlier up to around A.D. 700.

There does not appear to be any cultural or chronological overlap between Pecked Realistic and the following style, Pecked Abstract and Pecked Geometric. This suggests a gap between the end of Pecked Realistic and the beginning of Pecked Abstract and Pecked Geometric. The Pecked Abstract and Geometric styles are generally oriented horizontally on the panels, and the designs include curved lines, arches, circles, spirals, straight lines, crosses, and asterisks. Horizontal lines often connect other figures. There are perhaps Great Basin influences in these designs. Pecked Abstract began sometime after A.D. 700, succeeded by Pecked Geometric that ended around A.D. 1500.

Around A.D. 1500 incised rock art seems to have begun as a major style in the southern Hills. Sundstrom sees no overlap between the preceding Pecked Geometric and the incised styles, which again suggests a time gap and the

7-5 Modern vandalism surrounding a pecked human representation at 39FA7. (Linea Sundstrom)

infusion of a new culture. Painted styles, both Solid Painted Realistic and Triangular-Vertical, are thought to have begun about the same time. Some of the painted Triangular-Vertical glyphs (crosses, crescents, human handprints, and dots) may relate to Sioux sources around 1750-1850.

Sundstrom's work was not directed toward understanding the inherent meaning of the art. Some think of rock art as "talking pictures," but except for limited art documented from historic winter counts and similar sources, it is really going beyond the data to try to fathom the thoughts of the prehistoric artists.

Regardless of meaning, rock art holds a real value beyond the strictly scientific for those fortunate enough to view it. Standing in its presence can be awe-inspiring as one senses the depth of time and the human reality of the past.

Unfortunately, a certain minority lacks sensitivity to such things. Ignorance and in some cases malice have resulted in rock art defaced by carved initials, bullet holes, and worse forms of vandalism. How long can this precious resource survive the hand of modern humans?

References

On early Black Hills rock art studies:
Over 1941; Hughes 1959.
On recent Black Hills rock art studies:
Sundstrom 1984.

SUMMARY
8

The Black Hills have a prehistoric heritage covering many thousands of years, with contributions from numerous cultures, each adapted to its own time and place.

Paleo-Indian hunters, fortified with Asian traditions, laid claim to the unoccupied New World, settling in with their nomadic lifeways in the Black Hills and the surrounding prairies. Their livelihood depended on the big game of the terminal Pleistocene, the mammoth and giant bison.

With the close of the Pleistocene, the environment changed. The land dried in places and temperatures rose. Large Ice-Age beasts disappeared to be replaced by smaller game species. This marked the advent of the Archaic. The Archaic people's response to the climatic change was to more finely hone their foraging techniques. Many plant resources, perhaps earlier considered as only supplementary foodstuffs, appear to have been seriously sought as staples. Bison, where available, were still taken, but deer and rabbits became the primary targets for many of the hunters. This Archaic lifeway continued with minor changes for 6,000 years or more, earning the Archaic the distinction of being the longest cultural stage on the plains, if not in the entire New World.

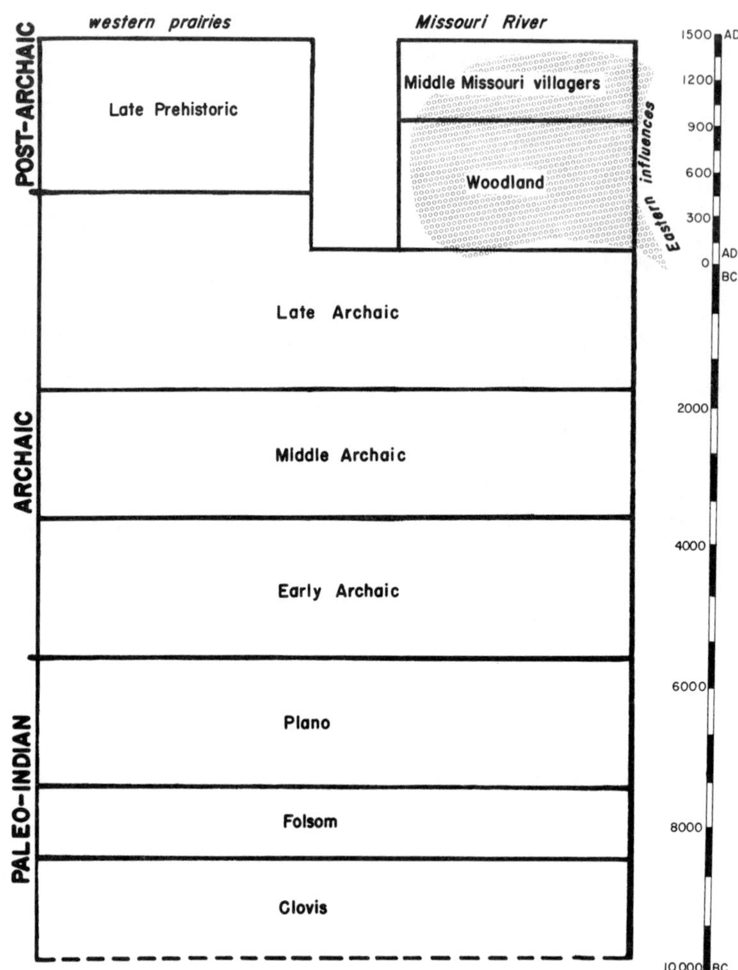

8-1 A prehistoric developmental scheme for the Black Hills and adjacent areas.

Following the Archaic, from about A.D. 500 on, the Black Hills were used primarily by hunter-gatherer groups of the Late Prehistoric. The period drew to a close only after the contact with Euro-American society from the east in the mid-1700s. These Late Prehistoric foragers maintained a mobile lifestyle similar to their predecessors, exploiting wild plant and animal resources whenever and wherever available.

However, these people did not live in a cultural backwater devoid of outside contact and influences during prehistoric times. Horticulturalists residing in Missouri River villages penetrated the Black Hills region, either living there for a time or influencing the locals in some other way. There is little evidence that they had any sort of widespread impact on the region. Although they must have wrought some change through their contact, the nature and extent of it is only a matter of speculation at this time.

The Black Hills contain the record of an incredible human journey through time. In its soil we can see the marvels of cultural adaptability, the persistence and drive necessary to sustain life with only stone-age technology.

Our insights into these times have made our lives richer, and yet what we know is still incomplete. Will there still be prehistoric remnants left to study and appreciate in the future, or will it all disappear as the result of selfish pothunting and vandalism?

References

On an overview of Wyoming archaeology:
Frison 1978.
On an overview of South Dakota archaeology:
Zimmerman 1985.

9-1 Wyoming's first State Archaeologist, George Frison. (George Frison and the *Northern Wyoming Daily News*)

BLACK HILLS ARCHAEOLOGY TODAY

9

Professionals in Government and Academia

The mid-1960s marked a watershed in professional archaeology in both Wyoming and South Dakota. Prior to that, South Dakota conducted a little archaeology through the South Dakota State Archaeological Commission (1947-1959), and there were some reservoir salvage excavations in both states funded by the federal government. Then the implementation of new federal and state cultural resource laws beginning during the 1960s allowed a dramatic increase in professional archaeological work.

The Wyoming legislature established the position of State Archaeologist in 1967, and University of Wyoming anthropology professor George Frison was chosen for the job. He held the position for 17 years until it was turned over to the present State Archaeologist, Mark Miller.

In 1973 the South Dakota legislature created its own position of State Archaeologist, and J. Steve Sigstad, then teaching at the University of South Dakota in Vermillion and acting as director of the W.H. Over Museum, assumed

9-2 Mark Miller became Wyoming State Archaeologist in 1984. (Mark Miller)

9-3 Bob Alex, South Dakota State Archaeologist, and his wife, Lynn, at the Smiley-Evans site.(Lynn Alex)

9-4 J. Steve Sigstad, South Dakota's first State Archaeologist. (Steve Sigstad and the *Yankton Daily Press and Dakotan*)

the position. Sigstad resigned in 1975 and was replaced by Robert Alex, the current State Archaeologist.

The State Archaeologist, working in conjunction with the State Historic Preservation Officer (S.H.P.O.), keeps track of archaeological work going on in the state and is liaison between developers, agencies, field archaeologists, and the lay public, assuring that the state's cultural resources are managed properly. On occasion the State Archaeologist's office may also be directly involved in surveys and excavations of sites, whether under a contract or strictly for research purposes.

There are a few academic archaeologists in the state universities, and in addition to teaching, they may engage in fieldwork and publishing. They are usually members of state, regional, and national societies, participating in annual meetings and maintaining contacts with colleagues.

Contract Archaeology

"Cultural resource management," a concept originating in the 1960s and vastly increasing in influence in the 1970s and on, has moved archaeological fieldwork another direction beyond the pure research generated in academia. Several significant pieces of legislation were passed that require archaeologists to become involved in early stages of projects on federal land or in federally-funded projects where alteration of the ground surface is likely to take place. Primary tasks of these archaeologists, conducting what was earlier known as "salvage archaeology" and now termed "contract archaeology," is to survey the land surface that may be "adversely affected" or "impacted," and record any sites present. Once found, all sites are mapped, photographed, and recorded on state site forms. They are then evaluated to see if they meet federally-stipulated criteria for inclusion on the National Register of Historic Places. If they do, then recommendations (e.g. avoidance, preservation, or excavation) and final decisions about the disposition of the significant sites are made by the land managing agencies involved and by the final authority, the Keeper of the Register. The current attitude in cultural resource management tends toward avoidance and thus conservatiion of prehistoric and historic resources whenever possible. This trend promises to continue for some time.

One of the results of the legislative mandates and their implementation by federal agencies has been a proliferation of jobs in archaeology, primarily involved in surveying land in advance of oil drilling, mining, timber harvesting, highway construction, and a variety of other ground-disturbing activities. This has in turn required additional archaeological personnel in the land managing agencies (United States Forest Service, Bureau of Land Management, Bureau of Reclamation, National Park Service) to oversee all of the contract work.

Contract archaeology has not been without its critics. Results of contract studies are seldom published in scientific journals, instead being incorporated into reports for limited in-house distribution. In addition, some work is done too rapidly, and quality had suffered. As in most professions, there are those whose workmanship leaves a lot to be desired.

Overall, though, contract archaeology has been responsible for the identification of thousands of sites that might otherwise have not been found, and the information yielded from them has been and will continue to be valuable to our quest of the past.

Avocationals

In addition to those employed by government, academia, and through contracts, there is a large heterogeneous body collectively known as avocationals. These are individuals whose professional ties are in other fields, although their love for prehistory involves them in archaeology to some degree during their spare time.

The Wyoming Archaeological Society, established in 1952, and the South Dakota Archaeological Society, established in 1969, arc the organizations that provide an ideal outlet for avocational energies in the states. They have regular local (chapter) meetings and annual state meetings, conduct surveys and excavations under the direction of professionals, and in the process, contribute a great deal to the knowledge of the region's prehistory.

Pothunters and Vandals

Regardless of the exemplary efforts of the Wyoming Archaeological Society and the South Dakota Archaeological Society and the positive opportunities they offer for archaeological pursuit among the lay public, there are those who have chosen other routes to self-fulfillment. These are the pothunters and vandals. Their motives vary, but the final results on the cultural resource base are about the same.

There are several types of individuals involved, including casual collectors, vandals, and commercial looters.

Casual collectors pick up artifacts as a recreational pursuit, perhaps involving the whole family on brief outings. There they scout out archaeological sites, collect their surfaces, and perhaps probe the ground with a shovel. They may resent professional archaeologists and legal prohibitions, although they will often profess ignorance of antiquities laws. Those items they recover from archaeological sites usually remain their personal possessions, often being framed behind glass and hung on their walls. They are primarily curio hunters and collectors, like antiquarians of old. They do not understand that the true value of artifacts is in their context in the sites, not in the objects themselves.

Vandals are an entirely different group. Rather than finding inherant value in prehistoric or historic remains and wanting to possess them, these individuals seek to damage or destroy remnants of the past, thus depriving future visitors any pleasure in their discovery. This may involve such things as pushing over log cabins from the 1800s, painting and carving names across rock art panels, firing weapons at the artistic representations of animals, or even applying chemicals to the walls to obliterate the prehistoric designs.

This type of behavior is senseless and quite difficult for law enforcement officers to stop.

Commerical looters form a particularly despicable, though at least an understandable, group. They have discovered that certain prehistoric artifacts have monetary value, and they seek to discover these "treasures" and then sell them to antiquarians who do not care how they were obtained.

Private land in Wyoming and South Dakota is exempt from antiquities laws, and pothunters can "mine" on such property without fear of personal liability. However, greed often drives them out onto the abundant federal lands where they can be arrested and prosecuted under both the 1906 Antiquities Act and the Archaeological Resources Protection Act of 1979.

Enforcement officers have been hired by various land managing agencies, and civil authorities, such as county sheriffs, have also become involved in trying to stem this tide of depredation on the heritage of the West. They are meeting with increasing success.

Summary

Archaeological activity in the Black Hills is relatively high, given the current demand for compliance work by contract archaeology. Areas that have never before felt the foot of an archaeological surveyor are now being walked and studied, and the files of the Wyoming and South Dakota State Archaeologists are growing rapidly with information on newly recorded sites.

Involvement in the Wyoming and South Dakota Archaeological Societies is strong, and the future of these organizations looks secure.

Unfortunately, the exploitation of archaeological resources for personal gain remains a problem as more people journey off asphalt highways in four-wheel drive vehicles.

Whether or not remnants of Black Hills prehistory will survive the coming years is difficult to say. Given adequate educational efforts directed at individuals at all age levels, a fair percentage of our population may become sensitized to the fragility of this non-renewable resource. Perhaps these people will join with the rest of us as stewards of the physical remains of our heritage, seeking to contribute to its preservation. Hopefully law enforcement agencies will be able to deal with the others who have consciously chosen to operate outside of legal and ethical boundaries.

Let us hope that future generations will be able to share the same wonder and appreciation of the past that we have been fortunate enough to experience.

References

On South Dakota archaeology history:
Helgevold 1981.
On pothunting, vandalism, and illicit antiquities trafficking:
Rippeteau 1979; Meyer 1973; Vitelli 1982; Brinkley-Rogers 1981; Hothem 1978; Reyman 1979; Sheets 1973; Williams 1977.

ARCHAEOLOGICAL AGENCIES AND INSTITUTIONS

South Dakota

State Agencies

State Archaeologist
South Dakota Archaeological Research Center
P.O. Box 152
Fort Meade, SD 57741
(605) 347-3652

State Historic Preservation Officer
State Historical Preservation Center
University of South Dakota,
216 East Clark
Vermillion, SD 57069
(605) 677-5314

Federal Agencies

Bureau of Land Management
(Dept. of the Interior)
State Archeologist
P.O. Box 30157
Billings, MT 59107
(406) 657-6090

Bureau of Reclamation
(Dept. of the Interior)
Regional Archeologist
Upper Missouri Region
P.O. Box 2553
Billings, MT 59103
(406) 657-6233

Corps of Engineers
(Dept. of the Army)
Regional Archeologist
7410 U.S. Post Office and Courthouse
215 No. 17th
Omaha, NE 68102
(402) 221-4133

State Archeologist
(Oahe Dam)
P.O. Box 670
Federal Bldg.
Pierre, SD 57501
(605) 224-8619

National Park Service
(Dept. of the Interior)
Regional Archeologist
Rocky Mountain Regional Office
655 Parfet
P.O. Box 25287
Lakewood, CO 80225
(303) 236-8675

United States Forest Service
(U.S. Dept. of Agriculture)
Regional Archeologist
Region 2
11177 W. 8th Ave.
P.O. Box 25127
Lakewood, CO 80225
(303) 236-9506

Forest Archeologist
Black Hills National Forest
P.O. Box 792
Custer, SD 57730
(605) 673-2251

Museums

Badlands National Monument
Visitor Center
Interior, SD 57750

Mammoth Site
Hot Springs, SD 57747

Mitchell Prehistoric Village
Mitchell, SD 57301

W.H. Over Museum
University of South Dakota
Clark and Yale Sts.
Vermillion, SD 57069

South Dakota School of Mines Museum
Rapid City, SD 57701

South Dakota State Historical Museum
Soldiers Memorial Bldg.
Pierre, SD 57501

Wind Cave National Park
Hot Springs, SD 57747

Organizations

Council of South Dakota Archaeologists (professional)
c/o Archaeology Laboratory
Augustana College
2032 So. Grange Ave.
Sioux Falls, SD 57105
(605) 336-5493

South Dakota Archaeological Society (avocational)
c/o Archaeology Laboratory
Augustana College
2032 So. Grange Ave.
Sioux Falls, SD 57105
(605) 336-5493

Wyoming

State Agencies

State Archaeologist
Department of Anthropology
University Station, Box 3431
University of Wyoming
Laramie, WY 82071
(307) 766-5564

State Historic Preservation Officer
Wyoming State Historic Preservation Office
Wyoming Recreation Commission
604 East 25th St.
Cheyenne, Wy 82002
(307) 777-7695

Federal Agencies

Bureau of Land Management
(Dept. of the Interior)
State Archeologist
P.O. Box 1828
Cheyenne, WY 82001
(307) 772-2074

Bureau of Reclamation
(Dept. of the Interior)
Regional Archeologist
Upper Missouri Region
(North Wyo.)
P.O. Box 2553
Billings, MT 59103
(406) 657-6233

Regional Archeologist
Lower Missouri Region
P.O. Box 25247
Denver, CO 80225
(303) 236-0684

Regional Archeologist
Upper Colorado Region
(SW Wyo.)
P.O. Box 11568
Salt Lake City, UT 84147
(801) 524-5447

Regional Archeologist
Pacific Northwest Region
(NW Wyo.)
Y.S. Courthouse,
Federal Bldg.
P.O. Box 043
Boise, ID 83274
(208) 334-1128

National Park Service
(Dept. of the Interior)
Regional Archeologist
Rocky Mountain Regional Office
655 Parfet
P.O. Box 25287
Lakewood, CO 80225
(303) 236-8675

United States Forest Service
(U.S. Dept. of Agriculture)
Regional Archeologist
Region 2
11177 W. 8th Ave.
P.O. Box 25127
Lakewood, CO 80225
(303) 236-9506

Forest Archeologist
(Wyoming)
c/o Medicine Bow National Forest
605 Skyline
Laramie, WY 82070
(307) 745-8971

Museums

Buffalo Bill Museum
836 Sheridan Ave.
Cody, WY 82414

Crook County Historical Society Museum
Sundance, WY 82729

Mammoth Visitor Center
Yellowstone National Park, WY 82190

Wyoming State Museum
State Office Bldg.
23rd and Central Aves.
Cheyenne, WY 82001

Organizations

Wyoming Archaeological Society (avocational)
c/o Milford Hanson
1631 26th St.
Cody, WY 82414

Wyoming Association of Professional Archaeologists (professional)
c/o Office of the Wyoming State Archaeologist
Department of Anthropology
University Station, Box 3431
University of Wyoming
Laramie, WY 82071

BIBLIOGRAPHY

Agenbroad, Larry D.
1977 *Mammoth site of Hot Springs, South Dakota.* The Caxton Printers, Ltd.
1978 *The Hudson-Meng Site: An Alberta Bison Kill on the Nebraska High Plains.* University Press of America.

Alex, Lynn Marie
1979 39BU2: A Fortified Site in Western South Dakota. *Newsletter of the South Dakota Archaeological Society* 9 (3): 3-7.

Alex, Lynn Marie, and Larry Zimmerman (eds)
1979 Phelps Collection Donated to South Dakota Archaeological Research Center. *Newsletter of the South Dakota Archaeological Society* 9(2):1-2.

Alex, Robert A.
1981 Village Sites Off the Missouri River. *In* The Future of South Dakota's Past (Zimmerman and Stewart, eds.). *Special Publications of the South Dakota Archaeological Society* 2.

Antevs, Ernst
1948 Climatic Changes and pre-White Man. *Bulletin of the University of Utah* 38 (20): 168-91.
1955 Geologic-Climatic Dating in the West. *American Antiquity* 20 (4, pt. 1): 317-35.

Baerreis, D.A., and R. Bryson
1965 Climatic Episodes and the Dating of the Mississippian Cultures. *Wisconsin Archaeologist* 46 (11): 143-48.

Benedict, James B.
1979 Getting Away From It All: A Study of Man, Mountains and the Two-Drought Altithermal. *Southwestern Lore 45 (3): 1-12.*
1981 Prehistoric Man, Volcanism, and Climatic Change: 7500-5000 ^{14}C Yr. B.P. *Abstracts with Programs* 1981, Geological Society of America 13 (7): 407.

Brinkley-Rogers, Paul
1981 The Big Business of Artifacts Theft. *Historic Preservation* 33 (1): 16-21.

Bryan, Alan L., and Ruth Gruhn
1964 Problems Relating to the Neothermal Climatic Sequence. *American Antiquity* 29 (3): 307-15.

Bryson, Reid, David A. Baerreis, and Wayne M. Wendlund
1970 The Character of late Glacial and Post-Glacial Climatic Changes. *In Pleistocene and Recent Environments of the Central Great Plains* (Dort and Jones, eds). University of Kansas, Department of Geology, Special Publications (3): 53-74.

Cassells, E. Steve
1980 Cultural Resource Investigations of the Hawkwright Timber Sale, Custer District, Black Hills National Forest, South Dakota. MS., Custer, S.D.
1981 Cultural Resource Survey of the Twin Sisters Timber Sale, Custer District, Black Hills National Forest, South Dakota. MS., Custer, S.D.
1982 Cultural Resource Survey of the Hospital Gulch Timber Sale, Spearfish District, Black Hills National Forest, South Dakota. MS., Custer, S.D.
1983 *The Archaeology of Colorado.* Johnson Books.

Cassells, E. Steve, David B. Miller, and Paul V. Miller
1984 Paha Sapa: A Cultural Resource Overview of the Black Hills National Forest, South Dakota and Wyoming. MS., Custer, S.D.
Clayton, Lee, W.B. Bickley, and W.J. Stone
1970 Knife River Flint. *Plains Anthropologist* 15 (50, pt. 1): 282-290.
Darton, N.H., and Sidney Paige
1925 *Central Black Hills Folio.* U.S. Geological Society, Bulletin 219.
Deetz, James
1967 *Invitation to Archaeology.* The Natural History Press.
Eckles, David
1978 Cultural Resource Survey of the Heeley Creek Timber Sale. MS., Custer, S.D.
Fagan, Brian M.
1975 *In the Beginning: An Introduction to Archaeology.* Little, Brown and Company.
Fredlund, Dale E.
1976 Fort Union Porcellanite and Fused Glass: Distinctive Lithic Materials of Coal Burn Origin on the Northern Plains. *Plains Anthropologist* 21 (73):207-11.
Frison, George C.
1974 The Application of Volcanic and Non-Volcanic Natural Glass Studies to Archaeology in Wyoming. *In* Applied Geology and Archaeology: The Holocene History of Wyoming (M. Wilson, ed.). *Geological Survey of Wyoming, Report of Investigations* 10.
1978 *Prehistoric Hunters of the High Plains.* Academic Press.
1984 The Carter/Kerr-McGee Paleoindian Site: Cultural Resource Management and Archaeological Research. *American Antiquity* 49 (2):288-314.
Frison, George C., Michael Wilson, and Diane J. Wilson
1976 Fossil Bison and Artifacts from an Early Altithermal Period Arroyo Trap in Wyoming. *American Antiquity* 41 (1):28-57
Froiland, Sven G.
1978 *Natural History of the Black Hills.* The Center For Western Studies.
Gant, Robert, and Wesley Hurt
1965 The Sturgis Archaeological Project: An Archaeological Survey of the Northern Black Hills. *South Dakota Museum News* 26 (7-8): 1-51.
Gries, J.P., and E.L. Tullis
1955 The Geologic History of the Black Hills. *In North Dakota Geological Society Guidebook*, South Dakota Black Hills Field Conference.
Groenfeldt, David
1978 Cultural Resource Survey of the Mayo Timber Sale. MS., Black Hills National Forest, Custer, S.D.
Hannus, Adrien
1984 The Lange/Ferguson Site, An Event of Clovis Mammoth Butchery with the Associated Bone Tool Technology: The Mammoth and its Track. Ph.D. Dissertation, University of Utah.
Haug, James K.
1979 Archaeological Test Excavations at Long Mountain, South Dakota. MS., South Dakota Archaeological Research Center, Ft. Meade, S.D.
Haynes, C. Vance
1974 Archaeological Geology of Some Selected Paleo-Indian Sites: *In* History and Prehistory of the Lubbock Lake Site (C.C. Black, ed.). *The Museum Journal* 15. West Texas Museum Association.
Helgevold, Mary Keepers
1981 A History of South Dakota Archaeology. *Special Publication of the South Dakota Archaeological Society* 3.
Hester, James J., and James Grady
1982 *Introduction to Archaeology.* Holt, Rinehart and Winston.
Hester, Thomas R., Robert F. Heizer, and John A. Graham
1975 *Field Methods in Archaeology.* Mayfield Publishing Co.
Hothem, Lar
1978 Indian Artifacting. *Fur-Fish-Game*, August: 26-40.

Hughes, Jack T.
1949 Investigations in Western South Dakota and Northwestern Wyoming. *American Antiquity* 14 (4):266-327.
Hughes, Jack T., and Theodore E. White
n.d. The Long Site: An Ancient Camp in Southwestern South Dakota. MS., Midwest Archeological Center, Lincoln, Neb.
Hurt, Wesley R., Jr.
1952 Report on Investigation of the Scalp Creek Site, 39GRI, and the Ellis Creek Site, 39GR2, Gregory Center, South Dakota. *Archaeological Studies Circular* 4, Pierre.
Jennings, Jesse D.
1968 *Prehistory of North America.* McGraw-Hill Book Co.
Johnson, James R., and James T. Nichols
1982 Plants of South Dakota Grasslands: A Photographic Study. *Bulletin 566, Agricultural Experiment Station, South Dakota State University*, Brookings.
Joukowsky, Martha
1980 *A Complete Manual of Field Archaeology: Tools and Techniques of Field Work for Archaeologists.* Prentice-Hall, Inc.
Kluckhohn, Clyde, and William H. Kelley
1945 The Concept of Culture. *In The Science of Man in the World Crisis* (R. Linton, ed.). Columbia University Press.
Kroeber, Alfred L., and Clyde Kluckhohn
1952 Culture: A Critical Review of Concepts and Definitions. *Papers of the Peabody Museum of American Archaeology and Ethnology* 47 (1).
Laughlin, W.S.
1967 Human Migration and Permanent Occupation in the Bering Strait Area. *In The Bering Land Bridge* (D. Hopkins, ed.). Stanford University Press.
Leamer, Donald J.
1971 Introduction to Middle Missouri Archaeology. *Anthropological Papers* 1, National Park Service.
Martin, Paul Schultz, and Peter J. Mehringer
1965 Pleistocene Pollen Analysis and Biogeography of the Southwest. In *The Quaternary of the United States* (Wright and Frey, eds.). Princeton University Press.
Meleen, Elmer E., and James J. Pruitt, Jr.
1941 A Preliminary Report on Rock Shelters in Fall River County, South Dakota. MS., W.H. Over Museum.
Meyer, Karl
1973 *The Plundered Past.* Atheneum Press.
Moorehead, Warren K.
1928 Explorations of 1922, 1924 and 1927. *In* The Cahokia Mounds, pt. 1, *University of Illinois Bulletin* 26 (4): 7-106.
Müller-Beck, H.
1967 On Migrations of Hunters Across the Bering Land Bridge in the Upper Pleistocene. *In The Bering Land Bridge* (D. Hopkins, ed.). Stanford University Press.
Mulloy, William T.
1954 The McKean Site in Northeastern Wyoming. *Southwestern Journal of Anthropology* 10 (4): 432-60.
1958 A Preliminary Historical Outline for the Northwestern Plains. *University of Wyoming Publications in Science* 22 (1).
Neuman, R.W.
1975 The Sonota Complex and Associated Sites on the Northern Plains. *Nebraska State Historical Society Publications in Anthropology* 6.
Over, W.H.
1941 Indian Picture Writing in South Dakota. *Archaeological Studies Circular IV.* University of South Dakota Musuem.
Pettingill, O.S., and Nathaniel R. Whitney, Jr.
1965 *Birds of the Black Hills.* Special Publication 1, Cornell Laboratory of Ornithology, Ithaca.

Reher, Charles A., and George C. Frison
1980 The Vore Site, 48CK302: A Stratified Buffalo Jump in the Wyoming Black Hills. *Plains Anthropologist* 25 (88, pt. 2, Memoir 16).
Reyman, Jonathan E.
1979 Vandalism and Site Destruction at some National Parks and Monuments: A Call for Action. *A.S.C.A. Newsletter* 6:4-9.
Rippeteau, Bruce E.
1979 Antiquities Enforcement in Colorado. *Journal of Field Archaeology* 6 (1):84-103.
Sheets, Payson D.
1973 The Pillage of Prehistory. *American Antiquity* 38 (3): 317-20.
Sigstad, J. Steve, and Joanita Kant Sigstad
1973 The Sisseton Mound: A Tribal Project. *Archaeological Studies Circular* 14. W.H. Over Museum.
Suess, H.E.
1965 Secular Variations of the Cosmic-Ray Produced Carbon-14 in the Atmosphere. *Journal of Geophysical Research* 70.
Sundstrom, Linea
1984 Rock Art of Western South Dakota (sec. 2), The Southern Black Hills. *Special Publication of the South Dakota Archaeological Society* 9.
Tratebas, Alice M.
1976 Cultural Resources Survey of Deerfield Reservoir in the Black Hills, South Dakota. MS., Black Hills National Forest, Custer, S.D.
1978 Archaeological Surveys in the Black Hills National Forest, South Dakota, 1975-1977. MS., Black Hills National Forest, Custer, S.D.
1979 Archaeological Excavations Near Stone Quarry Canyon, Black Hills National Forest, South Dakota. MS., Black Hills National Forest, Custer, S.D.
n.d. Functional Variability and Settlement Locations in the Black Hills. Draft Ph.D. Dissertation, Indiana University.
Tratebas, Alice M., and Kristi Vagstad
1979 Archaeological Test Excavations of Four Sites in the Black Hills National Forest, South Dakota. MS., Black Hills National Forest, Custer, S.D.
Trigger, Bruce G.
1968 *Beyond History: The Methods of Prehistory.* Holt, Rinehart and Winston.
Turner, Ronald W.
1974 Mammals of the Black Hills of South Dakota and Wyoming. *Miscellaneous Publications* 60, University of Kansas Museum of Natural History.
Vitelli, Karen D.
1982 The ABC's of the Antiquities Market. *Early Man* 4 (1): 29-32.
Wedel, Waldo R.
1961 *Prehistoric Man on the Great Plains.* University of Oklahoma Press.
Wettlaufer, Boyd
1955 The Mortlatch Site in the Besant Valley of Central Saskatchewan. *Saskatchewan Museum of Natural History, Anthropological Series* 1.
Wettlaufer, Boyd, and William J. Mayer-Oakes
1960 The Long Creek Site. *Saskatchewan Museum of Natural History, Anthropological Series* 2.
Wheeler, Richard P.
1952 A Note on the McKean Lanceolate Point. *Plains Anthropological Conference Newsletter* 4 (4): 39-44.
1954 Two New Projectile Point Types: Duncan and Hanna Points. *Plains Anthropologist* 1: 7-14.
Williams, Lance R.
1977 Vandalism to Cultural Resources of the Rocky Mountain West. M.A. Thesis, Colorado State University.
Zimmerman, Larry J.
1985 *Peoples of Prehistoric South Dakota.* University of Nebraska Press.

INDEX